Celebrating Sunday
for Catholic Families
2013–2014

Margaret M. Brennan

LITURGY
TRAINING
PUBLICATIONS

Nihil Obstat
Very Reverend Daniel A. Smilanic, JCD
Vicar for Canonical Services
Archdiocese of Chicago
February 26, 2013

Imprimatur
Reverend Monsignor
John F. Canary, STL, DMIN
Vicar General
Archdiocese of Chicago
February 26, 2013

Author: Margaret M. Brennan

Cover illustration by Eleanor Davis © LTP.

As a publisher, LTP works toward responsible stewardship of the environment. Visit www.LTP.org/environment to learn more about how this book was manufactured.

CELEBRATING SUNDAY FOR CATHOLIC FAMILIES 2013–2014 © 2013 Archdiocese of Chicago: Liturgy Training Publications, 3949 South Racine Avenue, Chicago IL 60609. Phone 1-800-933-1800; fax: 1-800-933-7094; e-mail orders@ltp.org; website www.LTP.org. All rights reserved.

ISBN 978-1-61671-127-6

CSCF14

"You shall love the LORD your God with all your heart, and with all your soul, and with all your might. Keep these words that I am commanding to you today in your heart. Recite them to your children and talk about them when you are at home and when you are away, when you lie down and when you rise."

(Deuteronomy 6:5–7)

Contents

How to Use

Celebrating Sunday for Catholic Families

This small weekly guide draws on the Gospel for each Sunday and Holyday for the coming year. It is intended to help parents engage their children (ages 8 and up) with the Mass and deepen their appreciation of the richness of their faith life. So often, going to Mass becomes a weekly event that begins and ends at the church door. The brief reflection for the parent on an excerpt from the Gospel is intended to spark his or her thinking about the Scripture that will lead to conversation with the family on the way to and from Mass. Suggestions for questions and conversation starters are provided, as well as some practice or practical way to carry this reflection into the life of the family.

We hope that many of the reflections and suggestions will enrich your family's life of faith. Some weeks, you may have other needs, concerns, or ideas that fit your life. If so, engage your children with those. A note about very young children: They are very able to enter into the liturgy through their senses. Singing the hymns, calling their attention to the changing colors of the liturgical seasons, and sitting where they can observe the gestures of the Mass are all ways to form them in the faith. Always remember, as the Rite of Baptism proclaims, you, as parents, are your children's first and most important teachers.

Twenty-third Sunday in Ordinary Time

Hearing the Word

Luke 14:25–33

In the name of the Father, and of the Son, and of the Holy Spirit.

Great crowds were traveling with Jesus, and he turned and addressed them, "If any one comes to me without hating his father and mother, wife and children, brothers and sisters, and even his own life, he cannot be my disciple. Whoever does not carry his own cross and come after me cannot be my disciple. Which of you wishing to construct a tower does not first sit down and calculate the cost to see if there is enough for its completion? Otherwise, after laying the foundation and finding himself unable to finish the work the onlookers should laugh at him and say, 'This one began to build but did not have the resources to finish.' Or what king marching into battle would not first sit down and decide whether with ten thousand troops he can successfully oppose another king advancing upon him with twenty thousand troops? But if not, while he is still far away, he will send a delegation to ask for peace terms. In the same way, anyone of you who does not renounce all his possessions cannot be my disciple."

Reflecting on the Word

In today's Gospel, Jesus gives two practical examples of the wisdom and value of preparing for an important task. When we attend Mass each Sunday, we are building the foundation for our faith. By praying with the community, listening to God's Word in the Scripture, and receiving Holy Communion, we prepare ourselves for living fully our Christian life.

What are some ways in which you can prepare your family for Mass so that each person can participate fully and receive its grace and blessing?

......ON THE WAY TO MASS

After the Prayer of the Faithful, which is a part of the Liturgy of the Word, the Liturgy of the Eucharist begins with the Preparation of the Altar. Today, let's focus especially on what happens during this time of preparation.

ON THE WAY HOME FROM MASS ......

Discuss what you observed and heard during this part of the Mass. Why do you think it is called the Preparation of the Altar?

Living the Word

Sunday has been called the preparation for Monday. With your family, talk about what needs to be prepared for school, work, or other events in the coming week. Sometimes the best preparation is practical. We organize what we will wear; we pack our lunches; we complete our homework. Other times, we may need to prepare our minds and hearts. We ask: What is my attitude about what I will do this week? Can I think of opportunities to be patient or kind or generous? All of these practical and spiritual preparations are important to living as disciples, that is, as followers of Jesus.

September 15, 2013

Twenty-fourth Sunday in Ordinary Time

Hearing the Word

Luke 15:31–32

In the name of the Father, and of the Son, and of the Holy Spirit.

[The father said to the oldest son,] " 'My son, you are here with me always; everything I have is yours. But now we must celebrate and rejoice, because your brother was dead and has come to life again; he was lost and has been found.' "

Reflecting on the Word

This story is the third in a series of parables that focus on finding what is lost: the lost coin, the lost sheep, the lost son. In each, when what has been lost is found, there is great rejoicing. We all know what it is like to lose something and how much energy and attention we expend to find what is lost. We also know what it is like to be "lost," to be "cut off," or to be "out of right relationship." Sometimes we are in the position of the younger prodigal son who we will hear about in today's Gospel. At other times, we are more like the father who stands with open arms to welcome back his wayward child. With whom do you identify right now? Is there something in your family life, or in the life of the community, that needs to be restored in order to be whole?

...... ON THE WAY TO MASS

Today we will hear a story about a father and his two sons. Let's listen for what we learn about how God relates to us and also for some ideas about how we relate to each other.

ON THE WAY HOME FROM MASS ......

Did anything surprise you in today's Gospel? If so, why? Can we think of anything in our lives that is similar to this story?

Living the Word

The family is the first place in which we experience relationship. We learn to love, to forgive, and to celebrate in the context of our families. This week, have a conversation about the importance of family life. What does your family mean to you? What have you learned about love and forgiveness from one another?

September 22, 2013

Twenty-fifth Sunday in Ordinary Time

Hearing the Word

Luke 16:10–13

In the name of the Father, and of the Son, and of the Holy Spirit.

Jesus said to his disciples: "The person who is trustworthy in very small matters is also trustworthy in great ones; and the person who is dishonest in very small matters is also dishonest in great ones. If, therefore, you are not trustworthy with dishonest wealth, who will trust you with true wealth? If you are not trustworthy with what belongs to another, who will give you what is yours? No servant can serve two masters. He will either hate one and love the other, or be devoted to one and despise the other. You cannot serve both God and mammon."

Reflecting on the Word

The word *trust* derives from the root word for *confidence* and *fidelity*, and also *comfort* and *consolation*. Trust is foundational to life. A baby needs to be able to trust that his or her needs for food, clothing, and comfort will be met. If these are not, the child is not able to develop a healthy sense of self and will struggle with the basic human tasks of loving others and engaging in life. It is not hard to imagine how chaotic life would be, and how anxious we would be, if we did not trust one another. As adults, we need to trust that our lives are meaningful and that our actions matter. We also model for our children what it means to trust and to be worthy of trust. The interactions we have with one another in our families are the building blocks for developing trust.

. . . . . . ON THE WAY TO MASS

Depending on the ages of your children, ask them what trust means to them. Whom do they trust? Why?

ON THE WAY HOME FROM MASS . . . . . .

Can you think of times when someone has trusted you? How do we feel when someone trusts us? When have you trusted someone?

Living the Word

One of the ways in which we build trust with others is by being reliable: if we say we will do something, we do it. Is there something that you have been putting off but want or need to do? Perhaps it is writing a letter or calling someone. Or, perhaps it is visiting an older relative or friend. Maybe there is an assignment or task that you need to complete. See if you can think of something that you have promised but not yet done, and try to do it this week. Encourage your family members to do the same.

September 29, 2013

Twenty-sixth Sunday in Ordinary Time

Hearing the Word

Luke 16:19–22

In the name of the Father, and of the Son, and of the Holy Spirit.

Jesus said to the Pharisees: "There was a rich man who dressed in purple garments and fine linen and dined sumptuously each day. And lying at his door was a poor man named Lazarus, covered with sores, who would gladly have eaten his fill of the scraps that fell from the rich man's table. Dogs even used to come and lick his sores. When the poor man died, he was carried away by angels to the bosom of Abraham."

Reflecting on the Word

The scene that Jesus describes to the Pharisees, no less true today than in Jesus's time, illustrates what has been called God's "preferential option for the poor." To understand what this means, we need to consider the Church's social teachings. In 1986, in "Economic Justice for All," the U.S. Catholic bishops wrote, "Jesus takes the side of those most in need. As followers of Christ, we are challenged to make a fundamental 'option for the poor'—to speak for the voiceless, to defend the defenseless, to assess life styles, policies, and social institutions in terms of their impact on the poor" (16). In 2005, Pope Benedict, in his encyclical *Deus Caritas Est* ("God Is

Love") wrote, ". . . love for widows and orphans, prisoners, and the sick and needy of every kind, is as essential to [the Church] as the ministry of the sacraments and preaching of the Gospel. The Church cannot neglect the service of charity any more than she can neglect the Sacraments and the Word" (22). In what ways does your parish strive to serve those who are suffering, whether from poverty, illness, or loss?

. . . . . . ON THE WAY TO MASS

Ask everyone to listen to the Gospel and to the Homily, and then to listen for where else in the Mass we pray for those who are suffering.

ON THE WAY HOME FROM MASS . . . . . .

Talk about what you have heard in the liturgy about serving those in need, and also look at your parish bulletin. What do you see that the parish is doing to respond?

Living the Word

During this next week, learn about a social service agency or group in your community. It may be a food pantry or home-less shelter, or a hospital or prison. While we can't do every-thing, each of us can do something to help those who are in need. Have a family conversation to see what your children would like to know more about and discuss whether this is something you can do. If this isn't the right time for you, put a note or picture on your refrigerator to remind you to pray for those who are suffering.

October 6, 2013

Twenty-seventh Sunday in Ordinary Time

Hearing the Word

Luke 17:7–10

In the name of the Father, and of the Son, and of the Holy Spirit.

[Jesus said:] "Who among you would say to your servant who has just come in from plowing or tending sheep in the field, 'Come here immediately and take your place at table'? Would he not rather say to him, 'Prepare something for me to eat. Put on your apron and wait on me while I eat and drink. You may eat and drink when I am finished'? Is he grateful to that servant because he did what was commanded? So should it be with you. When you have done all you have been commanded, say, 'We are unprofitable servants; we have done what we were obliged to do.'"

Reflecting on the Word

Jesus's words may sound harsh to us. Today few of us have servants, and we are inclined to believe that good work should be rewarded. So, we need to think more deeply about what Jesus is teaching his disciples. The key may be in the last line: "We are unprofitable servants; we have done what we were obliged to do." Can there be a certain joy, a sense of "rightness," when we do our jobs well—whether it is the work of parenting, or of being a student, or at our workplaces? If we truly believe that the work we are doing has value in itself, then doing that work well, for the sake of the work itself and not some external reward, brings us a sense of deep peace and even joy. Helping children experience an interior sense of satisfaction with their work that is not dependent on another's praise or approval can help them to develop a trust in their own capacity and self-confidence that will serve them well. They learn to trust themselves rather than trying to please others. Could this be at the root of Jesus's words today?

......ON THE WAY TO MASS

Discuss the activities—both work-related and play—that each member of your family most enjoys.

ON THE WAY HOME FROM MASS ......

Continue the conversation that you started on the way to Mass. Now, talk about Jesus's comments about doing "what we were obliged to do." Ask each person what he or she feels is a personally important work or task.

Living the Word

It can be hard to break a habit of giving praise. This week see if you can distinguish encouraging versus praising your child. As a parent, observe your child's responses. While this may seem to be awkward or strained at first, reflect on this practice in light of Sunday's Gospel. How can each of us learn to do "what we are obliged to do"? As Catholic parents, we are shaping our children's spirits, their souls, by our interactions with them. Helping them to become the people they are called to be is one way in which we can contribute to the world.

October 13, 2013

Twenty-eighth Sunday in Ordinary Time

Hearing the Word

Luke 17:11–19

In the name of the Father, and of the Son, and of the Holy Spirit.

As Jesus continued his journey to Jerusalem, he traveled through Samaria and Galilee. As he was entering a village, ten lepers met him. They stood at a distance from him and raised their voice, saying, "Jesus, Master! Have pity on us!" And when he saw them, he said, "Go show yourselves to the priests." As they were going they were cleansed. And one of them, realizing he had been healed, returned, glorifying God in a loud voice; and he fell at the feet of Jesus and thanked him. He was a Samaritan. Jesus said in reply, "Ten were cleansed, were they not? Where are the other nine? Has none but this foreigner returned to give thanks to God?" Then he said to him, "Stand up and go; your faith has saved you."

Reflecting on the Word

What, we may wonder, inspired the one leper, a Samaritan, to return to Jesus to say thank you while the other nine continued on their way? Perhaps he had cultivated what has been called "an attitude of gratitude." More than politeness, real gratitude shapes how we engage our experiences: the people we encounter, the challenges we face, the joys and the sorrows of our lives; the fact of life itself. The Benedictine monk David Steindl-Rast suggests that "surprise" is the first step toward learning to be grateful (*David Steindl-Rast: Essential Writings*. New York: Orbis Books, 2010, p. 59). Children seem to possess the capacity to be surprised while we, as adults, often are so focused on the routine that we stop seeing the world with amazement. Could this be a reason why Jesus says, in another Gospel passage, that we must become like little children?

•••••• ON THE WAY TO MASS

In your own words, share the story of the healing of the lepers that will be read at Mass. Begin to wonder with your children why one leper returned to thank Jesus.

ON THE WAY HOME FROM MASS ••••••

Continue the conversation. Did anyone hear anything at Mass that helped him or her to understand why the one returned? Explore what each person is thankful for today. Does anything surprise you?

Living the Word

Each day this week, at dinner, or before going to bed at night, ask everyone to name one thing that they were surprised by today or one thing for which they are grateful. Perhaps even make a list and post it where everyone can read it. At the end of the week, look it over. Together you might say, "Thank you God, for . . . ."

Twenty-ninth Sunday in Ordinary Time

Hearing the Word

Luke 18:1–7

In the name of the Father, and of the Son, and of the Holy Spirit.

Jesus told his disciples a parable about the necessity for them to pray always without becoming weary. He said, "There was a judge in a certain town who neither feared God nor respected any human being. And a widow in that town used to come to him and say, 'Render a just decision for me against my adversary.' For a long time the judge was unwilling, but eventually he thought, 'While it is true that I neither fear God nor respect any human being, because this widow keeps bothering me I shall deliver a just decision for her lest she finally come and strike me.'" The Lord said, "Pay attention to what the dishonest judge says. Will not God then secure the rights of his chosen ones who call out to him day and night? Will he be slow to answer them?"

Reflecting on the Word

This parable of the "persistent widow," as she is sometimes called, is intended to help us understand prayer. Like gratitude, which we reflected on last week, prayer is also meant to be a way of life, something that is woven into our actions, our thoughts, and our feelings. How else could we "pray always without becoming weary"? Clearly there are defined times for praying, such as grace before meals, before bed each night, and at Mass on Sundays. Being faithful to these moments of shared prayer helps us to be mindful of our relationship to God at all times.

......ON THE WAY TO MASS

Ask your family members to share what prayer means to them. Listen to see if there are different understandings of prayer.

ON THE WAY HOME FROM MASS ......

Reflect on the widow. Why do you think she kept bothering the judge? What helped her to be so strong and persistent in her request? What does this teach us about prayer?

Living the Word

Create a small space in your home that suggests a place of prayer. This can be as simple as a statue and a candle or plant on a table, or a beautiful religious picture. If there are special needs that you and your family are remembering in prayer, write them down and place them in this space. These may be prayers for sick or elderly family members or friends, prayers for concerns in the community or our world, or prayers of thanksgiving for blessings received.

October 27, 2013

Thirtieth Sunday in Ordinary Time

Hearing the Word

Luke 18:9–14

In the name of the Father, and of the Son, and of the Holy Spirit.

Jesus addressed this parable to those who were convinced of their own righteousness and despised everyone else. "Two people went up to the temple area to pray; one was a Pharisee and the other was a tax collector. The Pharisee took up his position and spoke this prayer to himself, 'O God, I thank you that I am not like the rest of humanity—greedy, dishonest, adulterous—or even like this tax collector. I fast twice a week, and I pay tithes on my whole income.' But the tax collector stood off at a distance and would not even raise his eyes to heaven but beat his breast and prayed, 'O God, be merciful to me a sinner.' I tell you, the latter went home justified, not the former; for whoever who exalts himself will be humbled, and the one who humbles himself will be exalted."

Reflecting on the Word

Again this week, we focus on prayer. In this parable, Jesus seems to be saying that it is not the outer form but the disposition of the heart that matters. When talking to children about this parable, we might ask what was missing for the Pharisee. Clearly, the Pharisee tried to be good and he followed the rules. Why, then, does Jesus prefer the prayer of the tax collector? Might it have something to do with the Pharisee's comparison of himself to others? Is Jesus showing us that when we pray we can come to God in our need?

• • • • • • ON THE WAY TO MASS

Let your family know that this week's Gospel reading will teach us more about prayer, and summarize the parable for them. Ask your children to listen to the words and the actions of the Pharisee and the tax collector.

ON THE WAY HOME FROM MASS • • • • • •

Ask your children to describe what they heard in the Gospel. Explore their thoughts on the difference between the Pharisee and the tax collector.

Living the Word

Later this week, we will celebrate the Solemnity of All Saints. In preparation for this, talk with your children about their patron saints. If you have pictures of these saints, place them in your prayer space or on the wall. At mealtimes or before bed, you might pray a short Litany of the Saints, using the names of your family's patrons: "Saint . . . , pray for us." You can find examples of the Litany of the Saints on the Internet, if you would like to see a model.

Solemnity of All Saints

Hearing the Word

Matthew 5:3–12a

In the name of the Father, and of the Son, and of the Holy Spirit.

[Jesus said:] "Blessed are the poor in spirit, / for theirs is the Kingdom of heaven. / Blessed are they who mourn, / for they will be comforted. / Blessed are the meek, / for they will inherit the land. / Blessed are they who hunger and thirst for righteousness, / for they will be satisfied. / Blessed are the merciful, / for they will be shown mercy. / Blessed are the clean of heart, / for they will see God. / Blessed are the peacemakers, / for they will be called children of God. / Blessed are they who are persecuted for the sake of righteousness, / for theirs is the Kingdom of heaven. / Blessed are you when they insult you / and persecute you and utter every kind of evil against you falsely because of me. / Rejoice and be glad, / for your reward will be great in heaven."

Reflecting on the Word

The Beatitudes are a meditation on the reign of God. Read this Scripture passage slowly and see which one or two of the verses speak most deeply to you, or which one or two you ponder and wonder about. As you talk with your children about the Solemnity of All Saints, explore how we see the Beatitudes in action today. Who are the "poor in spirit"? The "peacemakers"? The "clean of heart"? Who is mourning? Who is suffering or being persecuted? Who is "thirsting for righteousness"?

● ● ● ● ● ● ON THE WAY TO MASS

Today we celebrate people who have been officially recognized as saints, that is, as holy women and men. Are there people living today who you think are saints?

ON THE WAY HOME FROM MASS ● ● ● ● ● ●

Why is it helpful to have models for how to live our lives? Ask if there are any saints about whom your children would like to know more.

Living the Word

The Internet provides quick and easy access to learning more about the saints: http://www.catholic-saints-resource-center. com/. On November 2, we celebrate All Souls' Day, or the Commemoration of the Faithful Departed. This is a wonderful time to remember family members who have died. Placing their pictures in your prayer space and telling stories about these loved ones helps children to realize that death is not the end, but the beginning of a new life. As St. John Chrysostom said, "They whom we love and lose, are no longer where they were before. They are now wherever we are."

November 3, 2013

Thirty-first Sunday in Ordinary Time

Hearing the Word

Luke 19:1–10

In the name of the Father, and of the Son, and of the Holy Spirit.

At that time, Jesus came to Jericho and intended to pass through the town. Now a man there named Zacchaeus, who was a chief tax collector and also a wealthy man, was seeking to see who Jesus was; but he could not see him because of the crowd, for he was short in stature. So he ran ahead and climbed a sycamore tree in order to see Jesus, who was about to pass that way. When he reached the place, Jesus looked up and said, "Zacchaeus, come down quickly, for today I must stay at your house." And he came down quickly and received him with joy. When they all saw this, they began to grumble, saying, "He has gone to stay at the house of a sinner." But Zacchaeus stood there and said to the Lord, "Behold, half of my possessions, Lord, I shall give to the poor, and if I have extorted anything from anyone I shall repay it four times over." And Jesus said to him, "Today salvation has come to this house because this man too is a descendant of Abraham. For the Son of Man has come to seek and to save what was lost."

Reflecting on the Word

Zacchaeus must have been like many people of Jesus's time who wondered, "Who is this man named Jesus?" Zacchaeus was an important person who, because he was very short, climbed a tree to be able to see Jesus. Yet if that was all that happened to Zacchaeus, it is unlikely that we would be hearing his story today. Note that it is Jesus who speaks first, even inviting himself to stay at Zacchaeus's home. And, as a result of his encounter with Jesus, Zacchaeus changes. Isn't this the way it always is with God?

......ON THE WAY TO MASS

Recall that when Jesus was on earth, he taught about the kingdom of God and he also healed people from illness and sin. This made people wonder about who he was. Listen to today's Gospel for one person's experience.

ON THE WAY HOME FROM MASS ......

Why, with all of the people lined up on the road to see Jesus, do you think that Jesus spoke to Zacchaeus?

Living the Word

If you have small children, they will enjoy the Zacchaeus song, which is readily available on the Internet. Just type "Zacchaeus Song," in a search engine and you will be able to listen to it with the verses and melody on a number of sites. Older children may want to search "Zacchaeus House" to see an example of how a Scripture story has inspired several Chicago deacons to open a house of hospitality for homeless men.

November 10, 2013

Thirty-second Sunday in Ordinary Time

Hearing the Word

Luke 20:34–38

In the name of the Father, and of the Son, and of the Holy Spirit.

[Jesus said:] "The children of this age marry and remarry; but those who are deemed worthy to attain to the coming age and to the resurrection of the dead neither marry nor are given in marriage. They can no longer die, for they are like angels; and they are the children of God because they are the ones who will rise. That the dead will rise even Moses made known in the passage about the bush, when he called out 'Lord,' the God of Abraham, the God of Isaac, and the God of Jacob; and he is not God of the dead, but of the living, for to him all are alive."

Reflecting on the Word

We are reaching the end of the liturgical year. From now until the First Sunday of Advent, when a new Church year begins, the Gospel readings focus on what is called "the end times." These readings are often harsh and difficult to understand. Unlike the writers of the Gospel, we no longer expect the end time to be imminent. One way to connect with the meaning of today's Gospel is to focus on our ancestors in faith: Isaac, Jacob, and Moses. Sofia Cavalletti, a founder of the Catechesis of the Good Shepherd, speaks of the "golden thread" that weaves together salvation history. The same God who inspired the faith of these Old Testament figures continues to work in our lives. Just as they were important to preparing for the coming of the Messiah, Jesus, so we are important to preparing for the coming of the kingdom of God, that time when God will be all in all.

. . . . . . ON THE WAY TO MASS

Explain that we are coming close to the end of the Church year, and will begin a new year with the First Sunday of Advent. In what way is this different from the calendar year or the school year?

ON THE WAY HOME FROM MASS . . . . . .

Was there something in the liturgy—the readings, the Homily, the prayers—that reminded us that we are ending the Church year? Are there any signs around us—in nature or elsewhere—that show the change of seasons?

Living the Word

This may be a good time to talk about seasons and cycles of time. It is late autumn, and in many places the trees will have lost their green. Although we are over a month away from it, signs of Christmas will be evident in shopping malls and on city streets. We live, it seems, in multiple time zones! For us as Christians, one of these time zones is the liturgical year. Becoming aware of the rhythms and cycles of the Church year helps us to stay connected to the "golden thread" of salvation history.

November 17, 2013

Thirty-third Sunday in Ordinary Time

Hearing the Word

Luke 21:8–12

In the name of the Father, and of the Son, and of the Holy Spirit.

[Jesus said], "See that you not be deceived, for many will come in my name, saying, 'I am he,' and 'The time has come.' Do not follow them! When you hear of wars and insurrections, do not be terrified; for such things must happen first, but it will not immediately be the end." Then [Jesus] said to [his disciples], "Nation will rise against nation, and kingdom against kingdom. There will be powerful earthquakes, famines, and plagues from place to place; and awesome sights and mighty signs will come from the sky.

"Before all this happens, however, they will seize and persecute you, they will hand you over to the synagogues and to prisons, and they will have you led before kings and governors because of my name."

Reflecting on the Word

Again this week, the Gospel is harsh in its description of the end time. We may think that it sounds similar to the time we are living in, with wars and natural disasters occurring around the world. The challenge for us, as it was for the people of Jesus's time, is to learn how to respond with a faith that is firm in its belief that destruction will not have the final word. This is a good time to listen closely to the Eucharistic Prayer of the Mass, the prayers the priest will say after we sing the "Holy, Holy, Holy." What words in the Eucharistic Prayer give us reason to hope?

...... ON THE WAY TO MASS

Depending on the ages of your children, you may begin a conversation with them about how faith helps us respond to crises. Ask them to listen for words in the Mass that give them hope.

ON THE WAY HOME FROM MASS ......

See what words, phrases, or ideas each person noticed in the Scripture, songs, and prayers. Explore what those mean.

Living the Word

If you have created a prayer space, this is a good week to begin to put away the pictures of deceased loved ones. If there are special needs or concerns in your family or community, write them down and place them in the prayer space. Always, there are areas of the world and our planet earth that need our prayerful attention and concern. These, too, can be noted on prayer cards or in a book.

Solemnity of Our Lord Jesus Christ, King of the Universe

Hearing the Word

Luke 23:35–43

In the name of the Father, and of the Son, and of the Holy Spirit.

The rulers sneered at Jesus and said, "He saved others, let him save himself if he is the chosen one, the Christ of God." Even the soldiers jeered at him. As they approached to offer him wine they called out, "If you are the King of the Jews, save yourself." Above him there was an inscription that read, "This is the King of the Jews."

Now one of the criminals hanging there reviled Jesus, saying, "Are you not the Christ? Save yourself and us." The other, however, rebuking him, said in reply, "Have you no fear of God, for you are subject to the same condemnation? And indeed, we have been condemned justly, for the sentence we received corresponds to our crimes, but this man has done nothing criminal." Then he said, "Jesus, remember me when you come into your kingdom." He replied to him, "Amen, I say to you, today you will be with me in Paradise."

Reflecting on the Word

On this last Sunday of the liturgical year, we celebrate Christ, the King of the Universe. When we speak of Jesus as King of the Universe, we are looking forward to the end of time when Christ will come again. At that time, all creation will reveal the glory of God. This may seem to be quite a contrast from the image of Jesus on the Cross that today's Gospel presents. Similar to last week, this juxtaposition of Jesus suffering on the Cross with Jesus, King of the Universe, draws us into the Mystery of Faith that we proclaim at Mass.

• • • • • • ON THE WAY TO MASS

Explain to your children that today we will celebrate the Solemnity of Our Lord Jesus Christ, King of the Universe. Invite them to think about what kind of king Jesus is.

ON THE WAY HOME FROM MASS • • • • • •

Recall the words of the Mystery of Faith that were proclaimed. You may want to refer to a missalette to read them again. What do those words tell us about the kind of king Jesus is?

Living the Word

This week in the United States, we will celebrate Thanksgiving Day. For many of us, this is a time of gathering with extended family and friends. We need to prepare our hearts, as well as our homes, to welcome (or to be welcomed). The image of Jesus, the King of the Universe, welcoming the criminal into Paradise reminds us of how essential hospitality is to the Christian life.

December 1, 2013

First Sunday of Advent

Hearing the Word

Matthew 24:37–44

In the name of the Father, and of the Son, and of the Holy Spirit.

Jesus said to his disciples: "As it was in the days of Noah, so will it be at the coming of the Son of Man. In those days before the flood, they were eating and drinking, marrying and giving in marriage, up to the day that Noah entered the ark. They did not know until the flood came and carried them all away. So will it be also at the coming of the Son of Man. Two men will be out in the field; one will be taken, and one will be left. Two women will be grinding at the mill; one will be taken, and one will be left. Therefore, stay awake! For you do not know on which day the Lord will come. Be sure of this: if the master of the house had known the hour of night when the thief was coming, he would have stayed awake and not let his house be broken into. So too, you also must be prepared, for at an hour you do not expect, the Son of Man will come."

Reflecting on the Word

We experience, indeed we sense, the shift to the season of Advent: the colors on the altar and the priest's vestments change, a green wreath with four candles is prominent in the worship space, and the music is more expressive of longing and waiting. We know we are preparing for the birth of Jesus.

Yet if we reflect on the Gospel, we might also ask, "How else does Jesus come?" "How am I preparing to recognize the in-breaking of the holy in my life, and in my family life?" "What do I need to do to prepare, not just for the celebration of Christmas, but to receive those moments of grace that come when I am busy with the tasks of life?"

. . . . . . ON THE WAY TO MASS

Explain to your children that we are beginning a new liturgical season, Advent. Ask them to notice at Mass what looks and feels different from last week.

ON THE WAY HOME FROM MASS . . . . . .

Ask your children what they observed to be different at Mass. Begin to talk about what you can do in your home to help you pray during Advent.

Living the Word

"Come Lord Jesus, come Lord Jesus, come and be born in my heart." This simple prayer/song can remind us that we are in a period of preparation, waiting, and longing. It can be said at the end of grace before dinner or when saying goodnight. Even if the world is rushing toward the celebration of Christmas, we can take a moment each day to focus our hearts on our desire for Christ to come into our lives.

December 8, 2013

SECOND SUNDAY OF ADVENT

Hearing the Word

Matthew 3:1–6

In the name of the Father, and of the Son, and of the Holy Spirit.

John the Baptist appeared, preaching in the desert of Judea and saying, "Repent, for the kingdom of heaven is at hand!" It was of him that the prophet Isaiah had spoken when he said: / *A voice of one crying out in the desert, / Prepare the way of the Lord, / make straight his paths.* / John wore clothing made of camel's hair and had a leather belt around his waist. His food was locusts and wild honey. At the time Jerusalem, all Judea, and the whole region around the Jordan were going out to him and were being baptized by him in the Jordan River as they acknowledged their sins.

Reflecting on the Word

Today's Gospel is a loud and clear warning for taking time to prepare. For the people of Israel to be able to recognize that Jesus was the Messiah, others had to come before him. These forerunners had to open the minds, hearts, and imaginations of the people so that they would be ready to hear Jesus's message. The prophet Isaiah, the Gospel reminds us, foretold of John the Baptist. And John the Baptist preaches and baptizes in preparation for Jesus. If we stop to think about this, we begin to realize how God slowly prepares his people over the course of a long time. Who are some of the other people who helped to prepare the way?

......ON THE WAY TO MASS

Find out what each member of your family knows about John the Baptist. Recall that he was the son of Elizabeth, the cousin whom Mary visited after she learned she was to have a child. John the Baptist and Jesus were cousins.

ON THE WAY HOME FROM MASS ......

Talk about some of the people who have helped prepare you in your faith life. These may be parents or family members, teachers, priests and sisters, or friends. If possible, tell a specific story of how someone helped you.

Living the Word

The Jesse Tree is a visual way to learn more about the men and women who, throughout salvation history, helped to prepare the way for Jesus. Jesse Tree ornaments (search "Jesse Tree Ornaments" on the web for ideas and templates) can be colored and hung on a branch to create a type of family tree of our ancestors in faith.

December 15, 2013

THIRD SUNDAY OF ADVENT

Hearing the Word

Matthew 11:2–6

In the name of the Father, and of the Son, and of the Holy Spirit.

When John the Baptist heard in prison of the works of the Christ, he sent his disciples to Jesus with this question, "Are you the one who is to come, or should we look for another?" Jesus said to them in reply, "Go and tell John what you hear and see: the blind regain their sight, the lame walk, lepers are cleansed, the deaf hear, the dead are raised, and the poor have the good news proclaimed to them. And blessed is the one who takes no offense at me."

Reflecting on the Word

In *The Mood of Christmas and Other Celebrations*, the early 20th-century theologian, Howard Thurman, reflects on "The Work of Christmas":

When the song of the angels is stilled,
When the star in the sky is gone,
When the kings and princes are home,
When the shepherds are back with their flocks,

The work of Christmas begins:

To find the lost,
To heal the broken,
To feed the hungry,

To release the prisoner,
To rebuild the nations,
To bring peace among people,
To make music in the heart.

From Jesus's response to John, we realize that Jesus saw his mission as one of restoration and healing. How can we understand Christmas in this way? Some years we may be the ones who feed the hungry or work for peace; other years we may be the ones who are lost and broken. In either case, we are held in this mystery of the Incarnation that Christmas celebrates.

...... ON THE WAY TO MASS

Today is the third Sunday of Advent, traditionally called Gaudete Sunday, from the Latin *gaudete*, which means, "rejoice." Ask everyone to listen for the word *rejoice* at Mass.

ON THE WAY HOME FROM MASS ......

What does it mean to rejoice? In what does each person rejoice this week?

Living the Word

During the week, reflect on the meaning of the word *joy*. Is it the same as happiness? The root of the word *happiness* is *hap*, meaning "chance or fortune." The root of *joy* is *gaudio*, meaning "rejoice" or "the source of joy." What is the source of joy for you? Can we experience joy, even when life is difficult? Observe your children to see what brings them true joy or peaceful contentment.

Fourth Sunday of Advent

Hearing the Word

Matthew 1:18–23

In the name of the Father, and of the Son, and of the Holy Spirit.

This is how the birth of Jesus Christ came about. When his mother Mary was betrothed to Joseph, but before they lived together, she was found with child through the Holy Spirit. Joseph her husband, since he was a righteous man, yet unwilling to expose her to shame, decided to divorce her quietly. Such was his intention when, behold, the angel of the Lord appeared to him in a dream and said, "Joseph, son of David, do not be afraid to take Mary your wife into your home. For it is through the Holy Spirit that this child has been conceived in her. She will bear a son and you are to name him Jesus, because he will save his people from their sins." All this took place to fulfill what the Lord had said through the prophet: / *Behold, the virgin shall be with child and bear a son, / and they shall name him Emmanuel, /* which means "God is with us."

Reflecting on the Word

Probably the most overlooked person in the story of Jesus's birth is his foster father, Joseph. Without Joseph's cooperation, the birth of Jesus would have been very different. Today's Gospel reminds us of Joseph's courage, trust, and devotion. Willing to defy convention, Joseph took the pregnant Mary into his home and cared for her. The Gospel speaks of an angel appearing to Joseph in a dream. This will not be the only time that Joseph is guided to make important decisions by the visitation of an angel in his dream. How does the Holy Spirit guide us? How are we inspired to make decisions, especially decisions that require courage?

. . . . . . ON THE WAY TO MASS

Although Christmas is near, it is still Advent. Talk about the events that precede Jesus's birth, including the role of Joseph.

ON THE WAY HOME FROM MASS . . . . . .

Reflect on Joseph's courage. Explore what types of decisions or choices require courage.

Living the Word

By this time, most families are preparing to celebrate Christmas. Reflecting on Joseph's quiet, steady faithfulness may help transform the busyness of the days into our participation in what it means that God is with us.

Solemnity of the Nativity of the Lord

Hearing the Word

John 1:1–5, 9–11, 14

In the name of the Father, and of the Son, and of the Holy Spirit.

In the beginning was the Word, / and the Word was with God, / and the Word was God. / He was in the beginning with God. / All things came to be through him, / and without him nothing came to be. / What came to be through him was life, / and this life was the light of the human race; / the light shines in the darkness, / and the darkness has not overcome it. / The true light, which enlightens everyone, was coming into the world. / He was in the world, / and the world came to be through him, / but the world did not know him. / He came to what was his own, / but his own people did not accept him. /

And the Word became flesh / and made his dwelling among us, / and we saw his glory, / the glory as of the Father's only Son, / full of grace and truth.

Reflecting on the Word

If you have gone to Mass on Christmas Eve, you will have heard a different Gospel than this. Meditate on and savor this Gospel passage throughout the week. We can choose just about any sentence to ponder, so rich is this text from John.

...... ON THE WAY TO MASS

Now is the time for celebration! Ask your children to observe what changes they see in the church from just a few days ago.

ON THE WAY HOME FROM MASS ......

It is Christmas, and what better way to rejoice than to sing? Children usually pick up the hymns from Mass very easily or will know several carols. Join with them and sing.

Living the Word

There are good reasons that Christmas is celebrated over a period of time—at least until the Epiphany. One day can't really contain the fullness of this feast. Too often, we celebrate Christmas day and then we feel let down because it is over. This year, try to keep the spirit of Christmas alive and in focus by taking time to read Christmas stories, sing carols, and visit with friends and family throughout the season.

Feast of the Holy Family of Jesus, Mary, and Joseph

Hearing the Word

Matthew 2:19–23

In the name of the Father, and of the Son, and of the Holy Spirit.

When Herod had died, behold, the angel of the Lord appeared in a dream to Joseph in Egypt and said, "Rise, take the child and his mother and go to the land of Israel, for those who sought the child's life are dead." He rose, took the child and his mother, and went to the land of Israel. But when he heard that Archelaus was ruling over Judea in place of his father Herod, he was afraid to go back there. And because he had been warned in a dream, he departed for the region of Galilee. He went and dwelt in a town called Nazareth, so that what had been spoken through the prophets might be fulfilled, *He shall be called a Nazorean.*

Reflecting on the Word

Here is Joseph, again listening to the angel who comes in a dream, and doing what is best for Mary and the child Jesus. In this case, Joseph chooses to move his family to the town of Nazareth in Galilee, where he believes Jesus will be safe. In doing so, he also fulfills the prophecy that the Messiah will be a Nazorean.

Our children's safety and wellbeing is of paramount importance to us as parents. Did you know that of all the species, humans have the longest period of childhood? Children need the protection and care of their parents far longer than any other animal. We are entrusted with the most significant work: nurturing a young child from birth until he or she can be independent.

· · · · · · ON THE WAY TO MASS

Talk to your family about what they will hear in today's Gospel. Again, point out how important Joseph is to the story.

ON THE WAY HOME FROM MASS · · · · · ·

Today's Feast of the Holy Family of Jesus, Mary, and Joseph can be considered a patronal feast for all families. What are some unique qualities or characteristics of your family?

Living the Word

Every family has a story, a family history. As you gather with family over the holidays, ask the older members to share their experiences of Christmas when they were children. Or, start to make a family tree, even using pictures as well as names. Are there any special family traditions that you want to carry forward?

January 1, 2014

Solemnity of Mary, the Holy Mother of God

Hearing the Word

Luke 2:16–21

In the name of the Father, and of the Son, and of the Holy Spirit.

The shepherds went in haste to Bethlehem and found Mary and Joseph, and the infant lying in the manger. When they saw this, they made known the message that had been told them about this child. All who heard it were amazed by what had been told them by the shepherds. And Mary kept all these things, reflecting on them in her heart. Then the shepherds returned, glorifying and praising God for all they had heard and seen, just as it had been told to them.

When eight days were completed for his circumcision, he was named Jesus, the name given him by the angel before he was conceived in the womb.

Reflecting on the Word

It is New Year's Day, the beginning of a new year, and we celebrate the Solemnity of Mary, the Holy Mother of God. The Gospel account of the shepherds' visit to the infant Jesus reveals to us a mother who is listening intently to all that is said about her newborn baby and then reflecting quietly in her heart. An important part of the spiritual life is the ability to listen and to reflect on what we hear. Over the past few weeks, we have heard several accounts of Joseph listening to the angel in a dream, and now we hear of Mary, holding and reflecting on what she hears.

......ON THE WAY TO MASS

Recall that today we will hear about the shepherds' visit to the newborn king, Jesus. Explore what your children know about shepherds.

ON THE WAY HOME FROM MASS ......

Christmas is a time of wonder. Wonder with your children about what the shepherds might have felt and thought after seeing Mary, Joseph, and the baby.

Living the Word

We are still in the season of Christmas Time. With most of the festivities over, take time to reflect, like Mary did, on what the experience has been like for you and your family. In what moments did you feel that God was there with you? Were there surprising moments of joy? Was there too much to do and too little time to savor the moment? January invites contemplation as we live into this new year.

January 5, 2014

Solemnity of the Epiphany of the Lord

Hearing the Word

Matthew 2:1–2, 9–12

In the name of the Father, and of the Son, and of the Holy Spirit.

When Jesus was born in Bethlehem of Judea, in the days of King Herod, behold, magi from the east arrived in Jerusalem, saying, "Where is the newborn king of the Jews? We saw his star at its rising and have come to do him homage." . . . After their audience with the king they set out. And behold, the star that they had seen at its rising preceded them, until it came and stopped over the place where the child was. They were overjoyed at seeing the star, and on entering the house they saw the child with Mary his mother. They prostrated themselves and did him homage. Then they opened their treasures and offered him gifts of gold, frankincense, and myrrh. And having been warned in a dream not to return to Herod, they departed for their country by another way.

Reflecting on the Word

The angels' song brought the shepherds to Jesus, and now a star is the guiding light for the magi. What do these "messengers," angels and stars, tell us about how we are to discover the divine? Wonder, the Jewish theologian Abraham Heschel said, is "the chief characteristic of the religious man's attitude toward history and nature" (*God in Search of Man: A Philosophy of Judaism*). To be spiritual, to have religious life, requires the capacity for wonder. As children, wonder seems natural; as adults, we may need to cultivate our sense of wonder. Perhaps this is an area where the little child may lead us.

•••••• ON THE WAY TO MASS

In today's Gospel, the three magi bring gifts to Jesus. Talk about what gifts each person in your family might bring to Jesus.

ON THE WAY HOME FROM MASS ••••••

Sing "We Three Kings" and any other carols, as we are now at the end of Christmas Time.

Living the Word

Focus on wonder. About what do you wonder? Take a walk, or gaze at the night sky. Spend some time asking "wondering" questions: ask your children what each one of them wonders about. Resist trying to answer their questions, and just experience what it is like to wonder.

Feast of the Baptism of the Lord

Hearing the Word

Matthew 3:13–17

In the name of the Father, and of the Son, and of the Holy Spirit.

Jesus came from Galilee to John at the Jordan to be baptized by him. John tried to prevent him, saying, "I need to be baptized by you, and yet you are coming to me?" Jesus said to him in reply, "Allow it now, for thus it is fitting for us to fulfill all righteousness." Then he allowed him. After Jesus was baptized, he came up from the water and behold, the heavens were opened for him, and he saw the Spirit of God descending like a dove and coming upon him. And a voice came from the heavens, saying, "This is my beloved Son, with whom I am well pleased."

Reflecting on the Word

As we begin Ordinary Time, we move immediately from the accounts of Jesus's birth to his baptism by John the Baptist. This moment marks the beginning of Jesus's public ministry. Before he begins the work of proclaiming the Good News of the kingdom of God, Jesus follows the custom of being baptized. His real commission, however, follows his baptism: the Spirit of God blesses him and he hears his Father both claim and delight in him. The words, "with whom I am well pleased" can also be translated, "in whom I delight." This is a gift that all parents can bestow on their children. To delight in our children is to bless them.

······ ON THE WAY TO MASS

Explain that today we begin the period of Ordinary Time, the time between the end of Christmas Time and the beginning of Lent. Ask your children to observe what is different in the church. What colors are the vestments?

ON THE WAY HOME FROM MASS ······

Talk with your children about what gives them confidence, that is, what helps them to feel good and capable about schoolwork, or sports, or any other activity that is important to them.

Living the Word

As you settle back into the routines of your family's "ordinary" time, note what pleases you, what gives you delight. Let your children know that you take joy in them. Are there little ways in which you can express this? Perhaps a note on a bed or in a lunch box, or maybe an extra hug?

January 19, 2014

SECOND SUNDAY IN ORDINARY TIME

Hearing the Word

John 1:29–34

In the name of the Father, and of the Son, and of the Holy Spirit.

John the Baptist saw Jesus coming toward him and said, "Behold, the Lamb of God, who takes away the sin of the world. He is the one of whom I said, 'A man is coming after me who ranks ahead of me because he existed before me.' I did not know him, but the reason why I came baptizing with water was that he might be made known to Israel." John testified further, saying, "I saw the Spirit come down like a dove from heaven and remain upon him. I did not know him, but the one who sent me to baptize with water told me, 'On whomever you see the Spirit come down and remain, he is the one who will baptize with the Holy Spirit.' Now I have seen and testified that he is the Son of God."

Reflecting on the Word

We often hear that faith is a gift, and indeed it is. Nevertheless, all of us need certain signs or confirmations that what we believe is true. John the Baptist, who had known Jesus all of his life, grew into his recognition that Jesus was indeed the Son of God, the Messiah for whom Israel was waiting. As you think about your faith journey, what particular moments have strengthened your faith? These may be major life events or simple moments of insight. For most of us, there is not just one experience, but a variety of different ones that have contributed to our growth in faith.

• • • • • • ON THE WAY TO MASS

Begin a conversation about each person's image or idea of who God is.

ON THE WAY HOME FROM MASS • • • • • •

Talk about some of the different ways in which we experience God's presence at Mass: in God's Word, in the gift of the Eucharist, and in the worshipping community.

Living the Word

Throughout the week, give thanks for the gift of faith and for the people and events that have contributed to it. Now that we are in Ordinary Time (named "Ordinary" from the word ordinal, meaning "to count" because the weeks in this period of time are numbered, or counted), make your prayer space reflect the season. A green cloth and/or green plant with a piece of beautiful religious art or a Bible remind everyone that faith is a part of our everyday lives.

January 26, 2014

Third Sunday in Ordinary Time

Hearing the Word

Matthew 4:13–17

In the name of the Father, and of the Son, and of the Holy Spirit.

[Jesus] left Nazareth and went to live in Capernaum by the sea, in the region of Zebulun and Naphtali, that what had been said through Isaiah the prophet might be fulfilled: / *Land of Zebulun and land of Naphtali, / the way to the sea, beyond the Jordan, / Galilee of the Gentiles, / the people who sit in darkness have seen a great light, / on those dwelling in a land overshadowed by death / light has arisen. /* From that time on, Jesus began to preach and say, "Repent, for the kingdom of heaven is at hand."

Reflecting on the Word

The understanding of Jesus as the Light recurs throughout Scripture. Matthew recognizes Jesus as the Light foretold by the prophet Isaiah, and Jesus refers to himself as the Light of the World (see John 8:12). At our Baptism, we receive the Light of Christ, symbolized by the lighting of an individual candle from the Paschal candle (which is blessed at Easter and is a sign of Christ's overcoming the darkness of sin and death by his Resurrection). We are named "children of the light" and are asked to keep the flame burning until our death, when we will meet Christ in his heavenly kingdom.

......ON THE WAY TO MASS

Talk about light. What are different forms of light? What does light do for us? What would it be like if we did not have light?

ON THE WAY HOME FROM MASS ......

Can we imagine a light that darkness cannot overcome? Why would Jesus be that light?

Living the Word

Pay attention to various sources of light this week: stars and sun, candles and firelight. Children love to sing the familiar "This Little Light of Mine." Sing it often and perhaps talk about how they are a light.

Feast of the Presentation of the Lord

Hearing the Word

Luke 2:25–32

In the name of the Father, and of the Son, and of the Holy Spirit.

Now there was a man in Jerusalem whose name was Simeon. This man was righteous and devout, awaiting the consolation of Israel, and the Holy Spirit was upon him. It had been revealed to him by the Holy Spirit that he should not see death before he had seen the Christ of the Lord. He came in the Spirit into the temple; and when the parents brought in the child Jesus to perform the custom of the law in regard to him, he took him into his arms and blessed God, saying: / "Now, Master, you may let your servant go / in peace, according to your word, / for my eyes have seen your salvation, / which you prepared in sight of all the peoples: / a light for revelation to the Gentiles, / and glory for your people Israel."

Reflecting on the Word

We hear of Jesus as "a light of revelation to the Gentiles." The old Simeon, a devout Jew who has been longing for the Messiah, recognizes that Jesus is a light, not just for Israel, but for all the world. Simeon's prayer, or Canticle of Simeon as it is sometimes called, at the end of today's Gospel, is also known as the *Nunc Dimittis*. Simeon's life-long desire to see the Messiah, the Savior, has been fulfilled and he now is ready to depart in peace. February 2 is also known as Candlemas, marks the fortieth day after Christmas, and is the mid-point between the winter solstice and the spring equinox.

• • • • • • ON THE WAY TO MASS

Ask your children to again listen for any mention of light.

ON THE WAY HOME FROM MASS • • • • • •

Are there elderly people in your life? Do you see them as wise?

Living the Word

In honor of Simeon and Anna, the old prophetess in the temple who also was praying for the coming of the Savior, spend some time with someone who is older. It may be a grandparent or neighbor. If no one is near, write a letter or call. In what way are the elderly sometimes a light for us?

February 9, 2014

Fifth Sunday in Ordinary Time

Hearing the Word

Matthew 5:13–16

In the name of the Father, and of the Son, and of the Holy Spirit.

Jesus said to his disciples: "You are the salt of the earth. But if salt loses its taste, with what can it be seasoned? It is no longer good for anything but to be thrown out and trampled underfoot. You are the light of the world. A city set on a mountain cannot be hidden. Nor do they light a lamp and then put it under a bushel basket; it is set on a lampstand, where it gives light to all in the house. Just so, your light must shine before others, that they may see your good deeds and glorify your heavenly Father."

Reflecting on the Word

This week continues the focus on light, with Jesus telling the disciples that they are the light of the world and that they must not hide this light, but shine it forth. The last line of the Gospel helps us to think of light in a different way. Jesus says that their light must shine so that others may see their good works and thus give glory to God. This is a reminder that our actions and our words can be forms of light, or conversely, of darkness. We might also consider how our attitude or interior disposition is a form of light. How can we be light for each other in our family life?

· · · · · · ON THE WAY TO MASS

Begin a conversation about what has gone well or made each
person feel good during the past week.

ON THE WAY HOME FROM MASS · · · · · ·

After having heard the Gospel reading, talk about moments or
experiences of light in your lives.

Living the Word

This week we will observe Valentine's Day. Although
St. Valentine has been removed from the official Church
calendar, the day retains the tradition of letting people know
that we love them. In addition to classroom valentines or
cards for family members, try to think if there are people who
may be overlooked and for whom a little note or card would
be a light to brighten their day.

Sixth Sunday in Ordinary Time

Hearing the Word

Matthew 5:21–22a, 27–28, 33–34a, 37

In the name of the Father, and of the Son, and of the Holy Spirit.

[Jesus said to his disciples:] "You have heard that it was said to your ancestors, / *You shall not kill; and whoever kills will be liable to judgment.* / But I say to you, whoever is angry with his brother will be liable to judgment.

"You have heard that it was said, / *You shall not commit adultery.* / But I say to you, everyone who looks at a woman with lust has already committed adultery with her in his heart.

"Again you have heard that it was said to your ancestors, / *Do not take a false oath, / but make good to the Lord all that you vow.* / But I say to you, do not swear at all. Let your 'Yes' mean 'Yes,' and your 'No' mean 'No.' Anything more is from the evil one."

Reflecting on the Word

If we look carefully at Jesus's words admonishing his disciples about how they (and we) are to live, we notice that Jesus shifts the focus from the action itself to the thought or feeling that precedes it. Is it possible that he is calling our attention to the significance and power of these thoughts and feelings?

Or take the command to "Let your 'Yes' mean 'Yes,' and your 'No' mean 'No.'" Even if we consider ourselves to be honest folk, if we are really honest with ourselves, most of us know that it is hard to be so clear and direct all of the time. The family is the best place to learn how to express ourselves clearly and truthfully.

• • • • • • ON THE WAY TO MASS

Note the words "oath" and "vow" that are in today's Gospel and explain what they mean. Begin a conversation about where they are used (in court, in marriage, and so on).

ON THE WAY HOME FROM MASS • • • • • •

Explore Jesus's directive to mean what we say. Is this easy? When can this be hard?

Living the Word

Give special attention this week to how you use words. Take some time to talk with your family members about whether they can speak honestly to friends, each other, and teachers. Talk about why truth and honesty are necessary to healthy personal and communal life.

Seventh Sunday in Ordinary Time

Hearing the Word

Matthew 5:38–48

In the name of the Father, and of the Son, and of the Holy Spirit.

Jesus said to his disciples: "You have heard that it was said, / *An eye for an eye and a tooth for a tooth.* / But I say to you, offer no resistance to one who is evil. When someone strikes you on your right cheek, turn the other one as well. If anyone wants to go to law with you over your tunic, hand over your cloak as well. Should anyone press you into service for one mile, go for two miles. Give to the one who asks of you, and do not turn your back on one who wants to borrow.

"You have heard that it was said, / *You shall love your neighbor and hate your enemy.* / But I say to you, love your enemies and pray for those who persecute you, that you may be children of your heavenly Father, for he makes his sun rise on the bad and the good, and causes rain to fall on the just and the unjust. For if you love those who love you, what recompense will you have? Do not the tax collectors do the same? And if you greet your brothers only, what is unusual about that? Do not the pagans do the same? So be perfect, just as your heavenly Father is perfect."

Reflecting on the Word

Today's Gospel calls us to stretch ourselves to do what is uncomfortable. Nelson Mandela once said, "If you want to make peace with your enemy, you have to work with your enemy. Then he becomes your partner." He was acknowledging that the work of peacemaking requires us to engage with those with whom we disagree. In family life, differences of opinion or ways of doing things can often lead to strife. Sometimes it is the people very close to us with whom we need to walk the extra mile.

......ON THE WAY TO MASS

Explore how you interact or avoid interacting with people with whom you disagree or whom you do not like.

ON THE WAY HOME FROM MASS ......

How did you understand Jesus's words? What would doing what he says in today's Gospel look like in your life?

Living the Word

Pay attention to how your family responds to disagreements and small squabbles. How is forgiveness expressed? Are family members able to say, "I'm sorry" when they have hurt one another?

Eighth Sunday in Ordinary Time

Hearing the Word

Matthew 6:24–33

In the name of the Father, and of the Son, and of the Holy Spirit.

Jesus said to his disciples: "No one can serve two masters. He will either hate one and love the other, or be devoted to one and despise the other. You cannot serve God and mammon.

"Therefore I tell you, do not worry about your life, what you will eat or drink, or about your body, what you will wear. Is not life more than food and the body more than clothing? Look at the birds in the sky; they do not sow or reap, they gather nothing into barns, yet your heavenly Father feeds them. Are not you more important than they? Can any of you by worrying add a single moment to your life-span? Why are you anxious about clothes? Learn from the way the wild flowers grow. They do not work or spin. But I tell you that not even Solomon in all his splendor was clothed like one of them. If God so clothes the grass of the field, which grows today and is thrown into the oven tomorrow, will he not much more provide for you, O you of little faith? So do not worry and say, 'What are we to eat?' or 'What are we to drink?' or 'What are we to wear?' All these things the pagans seek. Your heavenly Father knows that you need them all. But seek first the kingdom of God and his righteousness, and all these things will be given you besides."

Reflecting on the Word

Increasingly, we are realizing not only our dependence on the natural world for our physical wellbeing (clean water and air, healthy soil for food), but for our spiritual wellbeing as well. Today's Gospel reminds us that nature—the birds, the grass, and the wildflowers—is our teacher. No matter where we live, we have some access to the natural world, even if it is to simply look up at the sky. When confined in a concentration camp, the Jewish writer Etty Hillesum found strength in seeing the budding branch of a tree outside of her window. Paying attention to our natural surroundings reminds us that we are a part of a splendid and surprising universe, something much greater than most of us imagine.

• • • • • • ON THE WAY TO MASS

Call attention to the world outside: Are trees in bloom, or are the branches still bare? Is the grass green, or is there snow on the ground?

ON THE WAY HOME FROM MASS • • • • • •

Why would Jesus want us to consider the way in which the wild flowers grow or the birds are fed? Can we make a connection to our lives?

Living the Word

Ash Wednesday is this week. As your family considers how you will spend Lent, reflect on this Sunday's Gospel. Instead of, or perhaps in addition to, "giving up" something, is there something you can do to develop a better connection to the natural world or to be more ecologically responsible?

First Sunday of Lent

Hearing the Word

Matthew 4:1–4

In the name of the Father, and of the Son, and of the Holy Spirit.

At the time Jesus was led by the Spirit into the desert to be tempted by the devil. He fasted for forty days and forty nights, and afterwards he was hungry. The tempter approached and said to him, "If you are the Son of God, command that these stones become loaves of bread." He said in reply, "It is written: / *One does not live by bread alone, / but by every word that comes forth / from the mouth of God.*"

Reflecting on the Word

Jesus's time in the desert was a type of retreat for him. It was a time of prayer and fasting, a time of strengthening his spirit. The forty days of Lent can be a form of retreat for each of us. Over these next six weeks or so, we are invited to focus on our prayer, fasting, and almsgiving so that our spirits will be made strong. The image of stones versus bread reminds us that we need to give attention to what truly nourishes our lives, and Lent offers us that opportunity.

Ask everyone to pay attention to what is different in the church today. What color are the vestments? What is different in the environment or in the singing?

Reflect on the meaning of the changes that were observed at church. Note that the word Lent is from the Old English *lencten*, which meant "springtime," or "spring," which suggests that it is a time for new life to emerge.

Living the Word

Make your prayer table or prayer space reflect the Lenten season. Use a violet (purple) cloth or runner. Add some stones or bare branches, whatever might suggest a desert or barren place. Take some time at dinner or before bedtime to talk together about Lent as a time to strengthen our spirits. Are there some practices that you might do as a family?

March 16, 2014

Second Sunday of Lent

Hearing the Word

Matthew 17:1–5

In the name of the Father, and of the Son, and of the Holy Spirit.

Jesus took Peter, James, and John his brother, and led them up a high mountain by themselves. And he was transfigured before them; his face shone like the sun and his clothes became white as light. And behold, Moses and Elijah appeared to them, conversing with him. Then Peter said to Jesus in reply, "Lord, it is good that we are here. If you wish, I will make three tents here, one for you, one for Moses, and one for Elijah." While he was still speaking, behold, a bright cloud cast a shadow over them, then from the cloud came a voice that said, "This is my beloved Son, with whom I am well pleased; listen to him."

Reflecting on the Word

This is the second time that we hear of a voice from heaven speaking the words, "This is my beloved Son, with whom I am well pleased." Recall the first time was at Jesus's baptism, before he began is public work. How fitting that at this moment of Jesus's Transfiguration, before he will begin his journey to Jerusalem that will end with his Death, he is again so blessed by his Father. Jesus took only three of his disciples to the mountain to witness this revelation. Peter's initial response to erect tents for Jesus, Moses, and Elijah who had appeared with Jesus reflects the awe he felt. He wanted to build a place of worship. Yet, the words that they heard direct them to "listen." Sometimes, listening is the work of worship that is demanded of us.

......ON THE WAY TO MASS

Recall how we will hear God blessing his Son, Jesus, with the same words that were said at Jesus's baptism. See if anyone remembers the story of Jesus's baptism.

ON THE WAY HOME FROM MASS ......

Talk about what lies ahead for Jesus. Why is it important that Jesus shares this moment with three of his closest disciples?

Living the Word

Is it possible to build some time for listening to God into each day? Experiment with even a minute of silence. Children enjoy the "silence game," a Montessori exercise in which everyone tries to still their bodies and to be quiet for a brief period. Practice the silence game and see what responses you get. Don't give up; if it doesn't work the first day, try again the next.

March 23, 2014

Third Sunday of Lent

Hearing the Word

John 4:6–10

In the name of the Father, and of the Son, and of the Holy Spirit.

Jesus, tired from his journey, sat down there at the well. It was about noon.

A woman of Samaria came to draw water. Jesus said to her, "Give me a drink." His disciples had gone into the town to buy food. The Samaritan woman said to him, "How can you, a Jew, ask me, a Samaritan woman, for a drink?" . . . Jesus answered and said to her, "If you knew the gift of God and who is saying to you, 'Give me a drink,' you would have asked him and he would have given you living water."

Reflecting on the Word

This brief excerpt is from a much longer passage that is today's Gospel (John 4:5–42). If you can, look at the complete reading before Mass, as it is so rich in conversation and meaning. Notice that the woman is a Samaritan. Jesus often has significant encounters with people who are considered outsiders, foreigners, and second-class citizens. Yet he approaches her in his thirst. Fear, lack of trust, prejudice—all of these separate us from one another. We might wonder what we would discover if we approached someone we considered "the other." Is it possible that we are missing the chance for greater life?

Mention that on the next three Sundays we will hear rather long but very important stories from Jesus's life. Perhaps share that today's Gospel tells of Jesus's meeting with a woman who was considered an outsider.

ON THE WAY HOME FROM MASS ......

Explore the term "living water" as a symbol. What gives us meaningful life?

Living the Word

We are nearing the midpoint of Lent. Depending on where you live, signs of spring may be appearing. Bring this to your prayer space. Some possibilities include a budding branch (forsythia or pussy willow are good choices), or a bowl of water (keep it clean and fresh each day). Consider who is "the other" for you and your family. Perhaps do a little research on this group of people, or if possible, find a way to meet and talk together.

Fourth Sunday of Lent

Hearing the Word

John 9:1–3, 5–7

In the name of the Father, and of the Son, and of the Holy Spirit.

As Jesus passed by he saw a man blind from birth. His disciples asked him, "Rabbi, who sinned, this man or his parents, that he was born blind?" Jesus answered, "Neither he nor his parents sinned; it is so that the works of God might be made visible through him." When he had said this, he spat on the ground and made clay with the saliva, and smeared the clay on his eyes, and said to him, "Go wash in the Pool of Siloam"—which means Sent—. So he went and washed, and came back able to see.

Reflecting on the Word

Who among us is not blind in some way? Don't we all have "blind spots"? We are all a bit like the blind men in the Indian folk tale who encounter an elephant: each man thinks the part he can touch—the long nose, the tusks, the big ears, the leathery skin—is the whole animal (if you are not familiar with the tale, search for it on the web). The challenge is that usually we do not know what we are not seeing! It takes a bit of humility and honesty to admit that we all have partial vision. It is only when we have been healed of our blindness that we become aware of what we were missing.

Tell the tale of the blind men and the elephant.

ON THE WAY HOME FROM MASS ......

Wonder about what it would be like to not be able to see, and then to be able to see. How might the blind man's life have been changed?

Living the Word

Is there an idea or an issue about which you felt strongly but now see it differently? What contributed to the change of view or opened the possibility of a new understanding? Talk about this as a family. For young people, it may be a subject or an assignment in school. Sometimes it is a particular person or group of people that as we come to know them better, our views about them change. In what way is this a type of healing?

April 6, 2014

Fifth Sunday of Lent

Hearing the Word

John 11:17, 20–23

In the name of the Father, and of the Son, and of the Holy Spirit.

When Jesus arrived, he found that Lazarus had already been in the tomb for four days. Now Bethany was near Jerusalem, only about two miles away. And many of the Jews had come to Martha and Mary to comfort them about their brother. When Martha heard that Jesus was coming, she went to meet him; but Mary sat at home. Martha said to Jesus, "Lord, if you had been here, my brother would not have died. But even now I know that whatever you ask of God, God will give you." Jesus said to her, "Your brother will rise."

Reflecting on the Word

As we listen to this Gospel story of Jesus's raising of Lazarus two weeks before Easter, we might ask ourselves: Who in this story is like me? Am I like Mary and Martha, grieving the loss of someone I love? Am I like Lazarus, dead in some way and in need of new life? Am I like Jesus, consoling the grieving and giving hope? This Gospel reminds us that for Christians, death does not have the final word. Instead, death leads to new life. We do not deny the pain of death or the reality of grief, but in their midst, we hold fast to the promise that, like Lazarus, we too will rise.

Depending on where you live, is it possible to observe changes in the earth? Are there signs of spring?

ON THE WAY HOME FROM MASS ......

Recall the story of Lazarus, and explore when or how you have experienced life after death.

Living the Word

We all participate in the cycle of life—death—new life. Sometimes for new life to break through, something must die. Plant a few fast-growing seeds (grass or wheat seeds, for example). Notice how the seed must be buried in the dirt. Then, watch over the next week for the new green to sprout.

April 13, 2014

Palm Sunday of the Passion of the Lord

Hearing the Word

Matthew 21:1–11

In the name of the Father, and of the Son, and of the Holy Spirit.

When Jesus and the disciples drew near Jerusalem and came to Bethphage on the Mount of Olives, Jesus sent two disciples, saying to them, "Go into the village opposite you, and immediately you will find an ass tethered, and a colt with her. Untie them and bring them here to me. And if anyone should say anything to you, reply, 'The master has need of them.' Then he will send them at once." This happened so that what had been spoken through the prophet might be fulfilled: / *Say to daughter Zion, / "Behold, your king comes to you, / meek and riding on an ass, / and on a colt, the foal of a beast of burden." /* The disciples went and did as Jesus had ordered them. They brought the ass and the colt and laid their cloaks over them, and he sat upon them. The very large crowd spread their cloaks on the road, while others cut branches from the trees and strewed them on the road. The crowds preceding him and those following kept crying out and saying: / "Hosanna to the Son of David; / blessed is he who comes in the name of the Lord; / hosanna in the highest." / And when he entered Jerusalem the whole city was shaken and asked, "Who is this?" And the crowds replied, "This is Jesus the prophet, from Nazareth in Galilee."

Reflecting on the Word

Today we celebrate Jesus's entry into Jerusalem, and we begin this most holy of weeks. Our Lenten journey is coming to an end. Notice how the crowds ask, "Who is this?" This is a good question for us to ask, as well. Who do you believe Jesus is? Who is Jesus for you?

•••••• ON THE WAY TO MASS

Note that this is the beginning of Holy Week, and that we will begin our celebration of the liturgy with a procession and blessed palms.

ON THE WAY HOME FROM MASS ••••••

Talk about what changes you observed in the Mass: the red vestments, the reading of the Gospel before the procession, the tone and feel of the music, and the blessed palm branches.

Living the Word

Place the palms in the prayer space. Notice that we began Lent by receiving ashes (which were last year's palm branches burned into ash), and now we receive palms. Although this is a solemn week as we journey with Jesus through his Last Supper and his agony and Death on the Cross, we can begin to prepare for Easter by cleaning our homes and planning our Easter celebration.

April 20, 2014

Easter Sunday of the Resurrection of the Lord

Hearing the Word

John 20:1–8

In the name of the Father, and of the Son, and of the Holy Spirit.

On the first day of the week, Mary of Magdala came to the tomb early in the morning, while it was still dark, and saw the stone removed from the tomb. So she ran and went to Simon Peter and to the other disciple whom Jesus loved, and told them, "They have taken the Lord from the tomb, and we don't know where they put him." So Peter and the other disciple went out and came to the tomb. They both ran, but the other disciple ran faster than Peter and arrived at the tomb first; he bent down and saw the burial cloths there, but did not go in. When Simon Peter arrived after him, he went into the tomb and saw the burial cloths there, and the cloth that had covered his head, not with the burial cloths but rolled up in a separate place. Then the other disciple also went in, the one who had arrived at the tomb first, and he saw and believed.

Reflecting on the Word

Easter is a joyful celebration of the mystery of our faith: Christ has died, Christ is risen, and Christ will come again. At first, Mary thinks that someone has moved the body and runs to Peter and John. Yet after Peter enters the tomb and John follows him, we are told that John "saw and believed." How human of them to be confused, perhaps frightened, at first. Perhaps this is how grace works. If we are willing to seek Jesus, we will know the gift of new life, of resurrection.

•••••• ON THE WAY TO MASS

The mood should be different today. For six weeks, we have not said or sung the Alleluia, so break forth with a familiar verse on the way to Mass.

ON THE WAY HOME FROM MASS ••••••

Talk about how Easter is expressed in the liturgy and the church: what did you see, hear, smell, and feel that expressed the joy of the Resurrection?

Living the Word

If the weather is good, spend time outdoors this week. Enjoy the park, woods, or lake. Be open to signs of new life. Have the birds returned? Are flowers appearing? Bring signs of new life into your home and add them to your prayer space and table.

April 27, 2014

SECOND SUNDAY OF EASTER / SUNDAY OF DIVINE MERCY

Hearing the Word

John 20:24–29

In the name of the Father, and of the Son, and of the Holy Spirit.

Thomas, called Didymus, one of the Twelve, was not with them when Jesus came. So the other disciples said to him, "We have seen the Lord." But he said to them, "Unless I see the mark of the nails in his hands and put my finger into the nailmarks and put my hand into his side, I will not believe."

Now a week later his disciples were again inside and Thomas was with them. Jesus came, although the doors were locked, and stood in their midst and said, "Peace be with you." Then he said to Thomas, "Put your finger here and see my hands, and bring your hand and put it into my side, and do not be unbelieving, but believe." Thomas answered and said to him, "My Lord and my God!" Jesus said to him, "Have you come to believe because you have seen me? Blessed are those who have not seen and have believed."

Reflecting on the Word

How wise of the Church to have this Gospel on the Sunday after Easter. Many, if not most of us, experience times of struggle and questioning. Thomas had been a faithful disciple, yet in his grief at Jesus's Death, he doubted the Apostles' account of Jesus's appearance. Faith is a journey with turns and detours, not always a straight line. At times, our task is to be faithful to the journey.

......ON THE WAY TO MASS

For the next fifty days, we will be in the season of Easter Time. Talk about why it is good to have a lengthy period of time to grow into the meaning of this great feast.

ON THE WAY HOME FROM MASS ......

Ask family members for their suggestions of ways to celebrate Easter over the next six to seven weeks. Decide on what you can do as a family.

Living the Word

Continue to sing Alleluia and Easter hymns as your prayer before or after dinner. Keep fresh flowers on the table or in your prayer space. Young children enjoy arranging flowers, so give them this task.

May 4, 2014

Third Sunday of Easter

Hearing the Word

Luke 24:13–15, 30–32

In the name of the Father, and of the Son, and of the Holy Spirit.

That very day, the first day of the week, two of Jesus' disciples were going to a village seven miles from Jerusalem called Emmaus, and they were conversing about all the things that had occurred. And it happened that while they were conversing and debating, Jesus himself drew near and walked with them. And it happened that, while he was with them at table, he took bread, said the blessing, broke it, and gave it to them. With that their eyes were opened and they recognized him, but he vanished from their sight. Then they said to each other, "Were not our hearts burning within us while he spoke to us on the way and opened the Scriptures to us?"

Reflecting on the Word

When has your heart burned within you? Perhaps it was hearing a Scripture passage or a Homily. Perhaps it was a time of conversation with a loved one or friend. Perhaps it was when you were gazing at the night sky, or seeing a newborn baby. What truth was being revealed to you at that time? Faith concerns the heart as well as the mind, and grace abounds if we open our hearts and our eyes.

······ ON THE WAY TO MASS

Recall the Last Supper and Jesus's words of blessing and breaking the bread before giving it to his disciples. Listen for when you will hear these words today.

ON THE WAY HOME FROM MASS ······

Notice how the disciples recognized Jesus when he broke the bread. The priest also blesses and breaks the bread at Mass. Can we begin to see the connection between the Scripture and the liturgy?

Living the Word

Share a meal with friends or relatives and enjoy the company. Talk about why it is important to break bread together.

Fourth Sunday of Easter

Hearing the Word

John 10:7–10

In the name of the Father, and of the Son, and of the Holy Spirit.

Jesus said again, "Amen, amen, I say to you, I am the gate for the sheep. All who came before me are thieves and robbers, but the sheep did not listen to them. I am the gate. Whoever enters through me will be saved, and will come in and go out and find pasture. A thief comes only to steal and slaughter and destroy; I came so that they might have life and have it more abundantly."

Reflecting on the Word

What does it mean to "have life and have it more abundantly"? What life is Jesus talking about? These are good questions for us to meditate on: What gives me life? What is essential for me to be engaged fully with life? If we think of Jesus as the gate, what does the gate open for us? The Gospel suggests that we can go in and out of the gate and find pasture, or, we might say, abundance.

. . . . . . ON THE WAY TO MASS:

What are some of the words that Jesus has used to describe who he is? (Examples might include *Gate, Good Shepherd, True Vine, the Way*.)

ON THE WAY HOME FROM MASS ......

Talk about why Jesus had to use various images to explain who he was.

Living the Word

Today is Mother's Day in the United States. This holiday was first celebrated by peace groups who wished to honor the mothers whose sons had died in the Civil War. Make a list of all of the various ways in which mothers contribute to making our lives full and meaningful.

May 18, 2014

Fifth Sunday of Easter

Hearing the Word

John 14:1–7

In the name of the Father, and of the Son, and of the Holy Spirit.

Jesus said to his disciples: "Do not let your hearts be troubled. You have faith in God; have faith also in me. In my Father's house there are many dwelling places. If there were not, would I have told you that I am going to prepare a place for you? And if I go and prepare a place for you, I will come back again and take you to myself, so that where I am you also may be. Where I am going you know the way." Thomas said to him, "Master, we do not know where you are going; how can we know the way?" Jesus said to him, "I am the way and the truth and the life. No one comes to the Father except through me. If you know me, then you will also know my Father. From now on you do know him and have seen him."

Reflecting on the Word

Today's Gospel is from Jesus's farewell discourse to his disciples before his Death. We can hear his deep concern and love for those who have been with him during his ministry. He reassures them that, not only will he prepare a place for them, but that he will come back for them. Jesus's declaration that he is "the way and the truth and the life" is a summary of all of his teaching. If we ponder Jesus's words and learn from his actions, especially his interactions with others, we will know who God is.

......ON THE WAY TO MASS

Has someone you loved moved away or died? Talk about what it is like to say goodbye to someone we love.

ON THE WAY HOME FROM MASS ......

Reflect on how the disciples might have been feeling, and explore what we can know about God the Father from Jesus's life.

Living the Word

We are still in the Easter season. While Easter baskets may have been put away, try to keep some visible reminder in your prayer space or on the table. Continue to sing Alleluia with the grace before dinner.

May 25, 2014

Sixth Sunday of Easter

Hearing the Word

John 14:15–17

In the name of the Father, and of the Son, and of the Holy Spirit.

Jesus said to his disciples: "If you love me, you will keep my commandments. And I will ask the Father, and he will give you another Advocate to be with you always, the Spirit of truth, whom the world cannot accept, because it neither sees nor knows him. But you know him, because he remains with you, and will be in you."

Reflecting on the Word

It is worth noting how Jesus speaks of love before he speaks of keeping the commandments. When we love someone, we naturally want to do what is right and good for them. The great teacher St. Augustine said, "Love God and do what you will." He could say this because he understood that if we love God first, then our actions will flow from that love. This does not mean that we will never make a mistake or sin, but that if love is the foundation, then we will know our error and seek to change. Love is the foundation of family life: love is the source of marriage and of bringing children into the world. Love gives us the strength and energy to do what is needed each day.

What kinds of words or actions let you know when you're loved by someone?

ON THE WAY HOME FROM MASS ......

How is love expressed in your family?

Living the Word

Be intentional about saying "I love you" to family members, or find little ways to express your love, such as a note in a lunchbox or on a pillow, an extra hug, or a phone call.

May 29 / June 1, 2014

Solemnity of the Ascension of the Lord

Hearing the Word

Matthew 28:16–20

In the name of the Father, and of the Son, and of the Holy Spirit.

The eleven disciples went to Galilee, to the mountain to which Jesus had ordered them. When they saw him, they worshiped, but they doubted. Then Jesus approached and said to them, "All power in heaven and on earth has been given to me. Go, therefore, and make disciples of all nations, baptizing them in the name of the Father, and of the Son, and of the Holy Spirit, teaching them to observe all that I have commanded you. And behold, I am with you always, until the end of the age."

Reflecting on the Word

Jesus's final words to his disciples are a commission to continue his work in the world and an assurance of his presence with them always, even after he has ascended to the Father. How do we understand Jesus's presence with us? Certainly he is present in the Eucharist and in the Scripture. In what other ways do we feel his spirit?

......ON THE WAY TO MASS

Is there someone close to you who lives far away? If so, talk about how you still know that you are in relationship with that person.

ON THE WAY HOME FROM MASS ......

Explore how we know that Jesus is still with us. How do we feel or experience this in our lives?

Living the Word

Images are important reminders of people we love. That is why we carry photos in wallets and phones, or place them on our dressers, desks, or living room walls. Similarly, the presence of religious art in the home can be a way of remembering our relationship to God. Look for beautiful pictures (for example, of the Good Shepherd) or statues and place something in each child's room.

SEVENTH SUNDAY OF EASTER

Hearing the Word

John 17:1–5

In the name of the Father, and of the Son, and of the Holy Spirit.

Jesus raised his eyes to heaven and said, "Father, the hour has come. Give glory to your son, so that your son may glorify you, just as you gave him authority over all people, so that your son may give eternal life to all you gave him. Now this is eternal life, that they should know you, the only true God, and the one whom you sent, Jesus Christ. I glorified you on earth by accomplishing the work that you gave me to do. Now glorify me, Father, with you, with the glory that I had with you before the world began."

Reflecting on the Word

Today's Gospel is from John's account of Jesus's Ascension. To our ears, it may sound very abstract and difficult to relate to. Perhaps a key phrase is at the end of this excerpt, when Jesus speaks of the glory he had with the Father "before the world began." This leads us into the mystery of the Most Holy Trinity, which we will celebrate in a few weeks. For now, it is enough to meditate on the fact that Jesus, who walked the earth as a human being as one of us, is one with God, who is eternal, without beginning or end.

......ON THE WAY TO MASS

Ask everyone to listen carefully to the words, especially the beginning of the Creed, which we say after the Homily.

ON THE WAY HOME FROM MASS ......

Talk about what the Creed is and why we profess our faith each week. Can anyone see a connection between today's Gospel and the Creed?

Living the Word

Use the Apostle's Creed at the back of this book, or print a copy from the Internet. Read it together sometime during the week and talk about how it contains the essential beliefs of our Catholic faith.

June 8, 2014

Pentecost Sunday

Hearing the Word

John 20:19-23

In the name of the Father, and of the Son, and of the Holy Spirit.

On the evening of that first day of the week, when the doors were locked, where the disciples were, for fear of the Jews, Jesus came and stood in their midst and said to them, "Peace be with you." When he had said this, he showed them his hands and his side. The disciples rejoiced when they saw the Lord. Jesus said to them again, "Peace be with you. As the Father has sent me, so I send you." And when he had said this, he breathed on them and said to them, "Receive the Holy Spirit. Whose sins you forgive are forgiven them, and whose sins you retain are retained."

Reflecting on the Word

It is now fifty days since Easter Sunday, and we complete our celebration of Easter with Pentecost (*pente* means "fifty"). Notice that twice Jesus says, "Peace be with you" to the frightened disciples. And in the same encounter, he gives them the power to forgive sins. Sin is a rupture in our relationship with God, with others, and even with ourselves. It is difficult to experience peace when we are out of good or right relationship. Reflect on times when you have felt peace or have experienced forgiveness.

......ON THE WAY TO MASS

Again this week, we have the opportunity to see the connection between the Gospel and the liturgy. Tell your family members what Jesus says twice to the disciples and ask them to notice where they will say the same words in the Mass.

ON THE WAY HOME FROM MASS ......

Talk about what it is like to extend and to receive the greeting of peace.

Living the Word

Where do you experience a need for peace? Do you see a need for peace in your family or community? Do you see a need for peace in the world? Spend time talking about how we can be peacemakers.

June 15, 2014

Solemnity of the Most Holy Trinity

Hearing the Word

John 3:16–18

In the name of the Father, and of the Son, and of the Holy Spirit.

God so loved the world that he gave his only Son, so that everyone who believes in him might not perish but might have eternal life. For God did not send his Son into the world to condemn the world, but that the world might be saved through him. Whoever believes in him will not be condemned, but whoever does not believe has already been condemned, because he has not believed in the name of the only Son of God.

Reflecting on the Word

How important it is to remember that God sent his Son Jesus to the world because he so loved the world! At times, it may be easy to overlook all that is good and beautiful in the world. The news and events in our lives keep us focused on what is wrong, what is still in need of healing. Our task as Christians is to align our actions with Jesus, to make the world better so that it reflects God's intention for creation. Recall that when God created the earth and all that is in it, God saw that "it was good."

...... ON THE WAY TO MASS

Since Pentecost, we are in the liturgical season of Ordinary Time, and the color of vestments and altar decorations is green, the color of growth and new life. Observe these changes in the church.

ON THE WAY HOME FROM MASS ......

Ask your family members to share what they see and experience as good in their lives and in the world.

Living the Word

Caring for our earth is a way in which we express our love for God's creation. What are some of the ways in which your family can help to make the earth more beautiful?

Solemnity of the Most Holy Body and Blood of Christ

Hearing the Word

John 6:52–54

In the name of the Father, and of the Son, and of the Holy Spirit.

The Jews quarreled among themselves, saying, "How can this man give us his flesh to eat?" Jesus said to them, "Amen, amen, I say to you, unless you eat the flesh of the Son of Man and drink his blood, you do not have life within you. Whoever eats my flesh and drinks my blood has eternal life, and I will raise him on the last day."

Reflecting on the Word

Today we celebrate the Most Holy Body and Blood of Christ. In some places, this solemnity is marked by a procession and/ or Adoration of the Eucharist. The gift of the Eucharist deserves our special attention and gratitude. Just as we need to eat nourishing food each day to be healthy, so we need to partake in this sacred meal to grow spiritually. By receiving Christ's life in such an intimate way—eating and drinking—we become one. In one sense, this unity is a mystery. It is beyond our understanding. Yet, if we reflect on the essential acts of eating and drinking, we begin to appreciate just how close to us Jesus wants to be.

......ON THE WAY TO MASS

As you talk about this Sunday's celebration, consider how basic and essential eating is to life.

ON THE WAY HOME FROM MASS ......

We all know the expression, "You are what you eat." Reflect on what this means in terms of receiving Holy Communion.

Living the Word

Bake bread together this week—it can be either a yeast bread or a simple quick bread such as banana bread. Make a list of all of the different types of breads from different cultures.

June 29, 2014

Solemnity of Sts. Peter and Paul, Apostles

Hearing the Word

Matthew 16:13–19

In the name of the Father, and of the Son, and of the Holy Spirit.

When Jesus went into the region of Caesarea Philippi he asked his disciples, "Who do people say that the Son of Man is?" They replied, "Some say John the Baptist, others Elijah, still others Jeremiah or one of the prophets." He said to them, "But who do you say that I am?" Simon Peter said in reply, "You are the Christ, the Son of the living God." Jesus said to him in reply, "Blessed are you, Simon son of Jonah. For flesh and blood has not revealed this to you, but my heavenly Father. And so I say to you, you are Peter, and upon this rock I will build my Church, and the gates of the netherworld shall not prevail against it. I will give you the keys to the Kingdom of heaven. Whatever you bind on earth shall be bound in heaven; whatever you loose on earth shall be loosed in heaven."

Reflecting on the Word

Today's Gospel and the celebration of Sts. Peter and Paul provide us the opportunity to reflect on the meaning and role of the Church. By appointing Peter as the "rock," the foundation, of the Church, Jesus established the pattern for leadership. All popes since then are successors of Peter. By naming the "Church," Jesus also gave a clear message that our faith is to be lived in community. We need others to walk the journey of faith. We need others to be the transformative power that the Church can be in the world.

. . . . . . ON THE WAY TO MASS

Talk about the structure of leadership in the Church: Who is your pastor? Who is your bishop or cardinal?

ON THE WAY HOME FROM MASS . . . . . .

The pope is the head of the universal Church. Talk about his role and leadership.

Living the Word

Summer is a good time for visiting other parishes, whether on vacation or just other parishes in your city or community. Go to Mass at a different Church once in a while so that your children see both the unity of faith and also the distinct communities.

July 6, 2014

Fourteenth Sunday in Ordinary Time

Hearing the Word

Matthew 11:25–27

In the name of the Father, and of the Son, and of the Holy Spirit.

Jesus exclaimed: "I give praise to you, Father, Lord of heaven and earth, for although you have hidden these things from the wise and the learned you have revealed them to little ones. Yes, Father, such has been your gracious will. All things have been handed over to my Father. No one knows the Son except the Father, and no one knows the Father except the Son and anyone to whom the Son wishes to reveal him."

Reflecting on the Word

As adults, we puzzle over Jesus's words that what God has "hidden from the wise and learned," he has revealed to "the little ones." Surely this is not a disparagement of knowledge and study. So what or who is meant by the "little ones"? One interpretation is that he is referring to children; another is that Jesus is speaking of those who are without pretense or guile. In the same way that children depend on and expect parents or other adults to meet their needs, so is each of us a child before God. We all must rely on a power that is greater than we are, and that power is God's love and grace.

•••••• ON THE WAY TO MASS

Talk about why we call God "Father." What does that tell us about God? What does it tell us about ourselves?

ON THE WAY HOME FROM MASS ••••••

Recall that Jesus also referred to God as his Father. Do you think the use of a parent's relationship to a child helps us to understand our relationship to God?

Living the Word

Each Sunday we recite the Our Father together at Mass. This week, make sure that each person knows this prayer by heart. Perhaps even take time to reflect on a different phrase of the prayer each day.

Fifteenth Sunday in Ordinary Time

Hearing the Word

Matthew 13:1–9

In the name of the Father, and of the Son, and of the Holy Spirit.

On that day, Jesus went out of the house and sat down by the sea. Such large crowds gathered around him that he got into a boat and sat down, and the whole crowd stood along the shore. And he spoke to them at length in parables, saying: "A sower went out to sow. And as he sowed, some seed fell on the path, and birds came and ate it up. Some fell on rocky ground, where it had little soil. It sprang up at once because the soil was not deep, and when the sun rose it was scorched, and it withered for lack of roots. Some seed fell among thorns, and the thorns grew up and choked it. But some seed fell on rich soil and produced fruit, a hundred or sixty or thirtyfold. Whoever has ears ought to hear."

Reflecting on the Word

Jesus used elements from the ordinary lives of the people he spoke to—seeds, birds, soil—to share his message. In this parable, we can focus on the seed and the various conditions that affected the seeds' growth; or on the sower, who generously sowed abundant seed, letting it fall all over the place; or we can ask ourselves, what is the seed? The beauty and power of parables is that there are multiple ways to understand them, and we never really exhaust their meaning. Meditate on this picture in words and discover how it speaks to you.

...... ON THE WAY TO MASS

Explain what a parable is: a short, simple story to teach a spiritual or moral lesson.

ON THE WAY HOME FROM MASS ......

See who remembers what happened to the various seeds. Why would the sower throw seed so randomly?

Living the Word

A good way for children to meditate on Scripture, particularly the parables, is by having them draw the story. This week's parable could be done as a small book, with one page for each of the four different places the seed was thrown. Don't worry about explaining the meaning, just let your children draw the story.

July 20, 2014

Sixteenth Sunday in Ordinary Time

Hearing the Word

Matthew 13:24–30

In the name of the Father, and of the Son, and of the Holy Spirit.

Jesus proposed another parable to the crowds, saying: "The kingdom of heaven may be likened to a man who sowed good seed in his field. While everyone was asleep his enemy came and sowed weeds all through the wheat, and then went off. When the crop grew and bore fruit, the weeds appeared as well. The slaves of the householder came to him and said, 'Master, did you not sow good seed in your field? Where have the weeds come from?' He answered, 'An enemy has done this.' His slaves said to him, 'Do you want us to go and pull them up?' He replied, 'No, if you pull up the weeds you might uproot the wheat along with them. Let them grow together until harvest; then at harvest time I will say to the harvesters, "First collect the weeds and tie them in bundles for burning; but gather the wheat into my barn." ' "

Reflecting on the Word

Another parable for us to ponder! How true to life this one is: we do not always know what will work for the good and what will not. Sometimes we just have to do our best and trust that, in time, we will be able to see what is right and good, and to let go of what is not. This parable reminds us that sometimes life is ambiguous, that things are not always as clear as we would like. We might ask, what type of faith did this man have?

•••••• ON THE WAY TO MASS

Talk about times when members of your family have had their good efforts derailed by someone else. Or, if this seems too abstract, just tell the parable in your own words and remind everyone to listen for the story.

ON THE WAY HOME FROM MASS ••••••

Ask if there have been times when it has been difficult to know what is right or good to do. Can we relate to this sower?

Living the Word

Try a little weeding experiment this week in your own garden, or just with a patch of grass outside near the sidewalk. Is it easy or hard to distinguish the weeds from the grass? Is it easy or hard to pull up the weeds without disturbing the flowers or grass?

July 27, 2014

Seventeenth Sunday in Ordinary Time

Hearing the Word

Matthew 13:44–46

In the name of the Father, and of the Son, and of the Holy Spirit.

Jesus said to his disciples: "The kingdom of heaven is like a treasure buried in a field, which a person finds and hides again, and out of joy goes and sells all that he has and buys that field. Again, the kingdom of heaven is like a merchant searching for fine pearls. When he finds a pearl of great price, he goes and sells all that he has and buys it."

Reflecting on the Word

These two parables of the buried treasure and the pearl of great price are wonderfully rich images. Jesus is trying to help people understand the kingdom of heaven. The quality of joy and freedom that each parable expresses gives us a clue to what is meant by the kingdom of heaven.

Explore whether there is something that you would be willing to sell all that you have to possess. (There is no one right answer; this is meant to spark the imagination.)

ON THE WAY HOME FROM MASS ••••••

Reflect on the parables: How do you think these men felt when they discovered the treasure or the pearl?

Living the Word

Place a treasure box or a single beautiful pearl in your prayer space. Over time, these images help us to understand the parables with our hearts.

Eighteenth Sunday in Ordinary Time

Hearing the Word

Matthew 14:15–20

In the name of the Father, and of the Son, and of the Holy Spirit.

When it was evening, the disciples approached [Jesus] and said, "This is a deserted place and it is already late; dismiss the crowds so that they can go to the villages and buy food for themselves." Jesus said to them, "There is no need for them to go away; give them some food yourselves." But they said to him, "Five loaves and two fish are all we have here." Then he said, "Bring them here to me," and he ordered the crowds to sit down on the grass. Taking the five loaves and the two fish, and looking up to heaven, he said the blessing, broke the loaves, and gave them to the disciples, who in turn gave them to the crowds. They all ate and were satisfied.

Reflecting on the Word

What a wonderful story of the abundance that comes from sharing whatever we have! Many of us live with the anxiety that we will not have enough. Today's Gospel reminds us that our needs will be met, that our hungers will be satisfied, if we live in relationship. An old immigrant woman who did not have very much in the way of material possessions always greeted the family and friends who came to visit her with the words, "Sit down, whatever I have I share." Whether it was a cup of coffee or a cup of soup, everyone felt the joy of being cared for by her.

● ● ● ● ● ● ON THE WAY TO MASS

Begin a conversation about sharing. When is it easy to share? When is it difficult?

ON THE WAY HOME FROM MASS ● ● ● ● ● ●

Explore what each person believes happened so that five loaves and two fishes were able to feed such a large crowd. What do you think was the miracle?

Living the Word

Find and read the children's story "Stone Soup." Maybe even have a stone soup party where you ask several friends to bring something from their fridge for a soup or salad and share a meal.

August 10, 2014

Ninteenth Sunday in Ordinary Time

Hearing the Word

Matthew 14:26–31

In the name of the Father, and of the Son, and of the Holy Spirit.

When the disciples saw [Jesus] walking on the sea they were terrified. "It is a ghost," they said, and they cried out in fear. At once Jesus spoke to them, "Take courage, it is I; do not be afraid." Peter said to him in reply, "Lord, if it is you, command me to come to you on the water." He said, "Come." Peter got out of the boat and began to walk on the water toward Jesus. But when he saw how strong the wind was he became frightened; and, beginning to sink, he cried out, "Lord, save me!" Immediately Jesus stretched out his hand and caught him, and said to him, "O you of little faith, why did you doubt?"

Reflecting on the Word

Aren't we all a little (or a lot) like Peter? We venture forth in confident faith, yet when conditions shift, we become anxious and fearful. Can we hear a tone of reassurance in Jesus's words as he reached out his hand to catch Peter? "Why did you doubt?" is not a rebuke, but a reminder that God is present, always. It is as if Jesus was saying to Peter, "Did you really think that I would let you sink? Did you really think that I would fail you?"

· · · · · · ON THE WAY TO MASS

Tell the Gospel story in your own words and ask that everyone listen carefully to it and to the Homily.

ON THE WAY HOME FROM MASS · · · · · ·

Discuss what helps us deal with our fears.

Living the Word

Find a copy of the prayer poem "Footprints in the Sand" by Mary Stevenson. It is easily available online. Place it in your prayer space and read it together.

August 15, 2014

Solemnity of the Assumption of the Blessed Virgin Mary

Hearing the Word

Luke 1:39–42

In the name of the Father, and of the Son, and of the Holy Spirit.

Mary set out and traveled to the hill country in haste to a town of Judah, where she entered the house of Zechariah and greeted Elizabeth. When Elizabeth heard Mary's greeting, the infant leaped in her womb, and Elizabeth, filled with the Holy Spirit, cried out in a loud voice and said, "Blessed are you among women, and blessed is the fruit of your womb."

Reflecting on the Word

Today's celebration of the Assumption of the Blessed Virgin Mary is a day to honor the Mother of Jesus. In today's Gospel, we hear of her visitation to her cousin Elizabeth. Both women were unexpectedly expecting a baby, and we can imagine how reassuring it was for them to be together. Elizabeth's greeting to Mary is familiar to us, as we say it each time we pray the Hail Mary. And Mary's response to Elizabeth (which we will hear in the full Gospel at Mass—Luke 1:46–55) is a prayer called the *Magnificat*.

Explain what the word *assumption* means: At the end of Mary's life, God assumed her, body and soul, into heaven.

ON THE WAY HOME FROM MASS ......

Stop and buy some flowers for your prayer space, or gather them from the garden when you get home.

Living the Word

Because this feast takes place in mid-August when in many parts of the world, the harvest is at its peak, it was traditionally a time for blessing the fruits and grains. Take a trip to a farmer's market and enjoy the beauty and variety of fruits, vegetables, and flowers.

Twentieth Sunday in Ordinary Time

Hearing the Word

Matthew 15:22–28

In the name of the Father, and of the Son, and of the Holy Spirit.

[A Canaanite woman called out] "Have pity on me, Lord, Son of David! My daughter is tormented by a demon." But Jesus did not say a word in answer to her. Jesus' disciples came and asked him, "Send her away, for she keeps calling out after us." He said in reply, "I was sent only to the lost sheep of the house of Israel." But the woman came and did Jesus homage, saying, "Lord, help me." He said in reply, "It is not right to take the food of the children and throw it to the dogs." She said, "Please, Lord, for even the dogs eat the scraps that fall from the table of their masters." Then Jesus said to her in reply, "O woman, great is your faith! Let it be done for you as you wish." And the woman's daughter was healed from that hour.

Reflecting on the Word

As parents, we can identify with the mother's persistence on behalf of her suffering daughter. As a Canaanite, she would have been a foreigner, a second-class citizen, yet she did not hesitate to approach Jesus. The disciples plead for him to send her away, and Jesus initially seems to ignore her when he does not speak to her. Even with his attempt to dissuade her, she is strong and clear. Can this be an example of prayer for us? Whether or not we feel that we are being heard, it is our task to persist in prayer.

・・・・・・ ON THE WAY TO MASS

Are there some groups of people who are strangers or foreigners in your hometown or community? How are they treated?

ON THE WAY HOME FROM MASS ・・・・・・

How did the homilist explain this encounter between the Canaanite woman and Jesus?

Living the Word

Think of individuals or groups of people who are suffering, whether from illness, war, or poverty. Be intentional about praying for them. If there is some other way in which you can be helpful to them, try to do it this week.

Twenty-first Sunday in Ordinary Time

Hearing the Word

Matthew 16:15–18

In the name of the Father, and of the Son, and of the Holy Spirit.

[Jesus said to his disciples:] "But who do you say that I am?" Simon Peter said in reply, "You are the Christ, the Son of the living God." Jesus said to him in reply, "Blessed are you, Simon son of Jonah. For flesh and blood has not revealed this to you, but my heavenly Father. And so I say to you, you are Peter, and upon this rock I will build my church, and the gates of the netherworld shall not prevail against it."

Reflecting on the Word

We heard this Gospel in June on the Solemnity of Sts. Peter and Paul. As we listen to it again, we can focus on Jesus's question, "But who do you say that I am?" Answering this question is the lifelong work of the Christian. We are always in process, always understanding who Jesus is in new and deeper ways. Peter responds that Jesus is "the Christ, the Son of the living God." His recognition of Jesus as the Christ, the Anointed One, the Messiah, is a grace and gift from God, which will empower him to carry Jesus's message forward.

Talk a little about the Apostle Peter. What have we heard about him over the past few weeks?

ON THE WAY HOME FROM MASS ......

Summer is ending and the school year is beginning. Talk about how, just as we continue to learn more math and history, so we also continue to learn about our faith.

Living the Word

Make a list of all of the different names or titles for Jesus that you can think of. Place this list in your prayer space, or use it as a litany of prayer.

Twenty-second Sunday in Ordinary Time

Hearing the Word

Matthew 16:21–25

In the name of the Father, and of the Son, and of the Holy Spirit.

Jesus began to show his disciples that he must go to Jerusalem and suffer greatly from the elders, the chief priests, and the scribes, and be killed and on the third day be raised. Then Peter took Jesus aside and began to rebuke him, "God forbid, Lord! No such thing shall ever happen to you." He turned and said to Peter, "Get behind me, Satan! You are an obstacle to me. You are thinking not as God does, but as human beings do."

Then Jesus said to his disciples, "Whoever wishes to come after me must deny himself, take up his cross, and follow me. For whoever wishes to save his life will lose it, but whoever loses his life for my sake will find it."

Reflecting on the Word

Peter again! No doubt Peter believed he could protect Jesus from the fate Jesus was describing. But Jesus knew that he would suffer and so would all of his followers. The question of carrying our cross is a difficult one. None of us seeks pain, but the reality is that no one goes through life without suffering. How do we understand suffering in light of our faith? Do we believe that we can live the Paschal Mystery of death to new life?

······ ON THE WAY TO MASS

Are we able to acknowledge our suffering—little sorrows as well as great pain—or do we, like Peter, try to ignore the reality of suffering?

ON THE WAY HOME FROM MASS ······

Talk about how we can learn to be empathic to the suffering of others, and how we respond when we see pain and sorrow.

Living the Word

Do you know anyone who is suffering? Can you send them a note of comfort or offer them support in some way?

Everyday Family Prayers

The Sign of the Cross

The Sign of the Cross is the first prayer and the last: of each day, and of each Christian life. It is a prayer of the body as well as a prayer of words. When we are presented for Baptism, the community traces this sign on our bodies for the first time. Parents may trace it daily on their children. We learn to trace it daily on ourselves and on those whom we love. When we die, our loved ones will trace this holy sign on us for the last time.

In the name of the Father,

and of the Son,

and of the Holy Spirit. Amen.

The Lord's Prayer

The Lord's Prayer, or the Our Father, is a very important prayer for Christians because Jesus himself taught it to his disciples, who taught it to his Church. Today, we say this prayer as part of Mass, in the Rosary, and in personal prayer. There are seven petitions in the Lord's Prayer. The first three ask for God to be glorified and praised, and the next four ask for God to help take care of our physical and spiritual needs.

Our Father, who art in heaven,

hallowed be thy name;

thy kingdom come,

thy will be done

on earth as it is in heaven.

Give us this day our daily bread,

and forgive us our trespasses,

as we forgive those who trespass against us;

and lead us not into temptation, but deliver us
from evil.

The Apostles' Creed

The Apostles' Creed is one of the earliest creeds we have; scholars believe it was written within the second century. The Apostles' Creed is shorter than the Nicene Creed, but it states what we believe about the Father, Son, and Holy Spirit. This prayer is sometimes used at Mass, especially at Masses with children, and is part of the Rosary.

I believe in God,

the Father almighty,

Creator of heaven and earth,

and in Jesus Christ, his only Son, our Lord,

who was conceived by the Holy Spirit,

born of the Virgin Mary,

suffered under Pontius Pilate,

was crucified, died and was buried;

he descended into hell;

and on the third day he rose again from the dead;

he ascended into heaven,

and is seated at the right hand of God the Father almighty;

from there he will come to judge the living and the dead.

I believe in the Holy Spirit,

the holy catholic Church,

the communion of saints,

the forgiveness of sins,

the resurrection of the body,

and life everlasting. Amen.

The Nicene Creed

The Nicene Creed was written at the Council of Nicaea in 325 AD, when bishops of the Church gathered together in order to articulate true belief in who Christ is and his relationship to God the Father. The Nicene Creed was the final document of that Council, written so that all the faithful may know the central teachings of Christianity. We say this prayer at Mass.

I believe in one God,

the Father almighty,

maker of heaven and earth,

of all things visible and invisible.

I believe in one Lord Jesus Christ,

the Only Begotten Son of God,

born of the Father before all ages.

God from God, Light from Light,

true God from true God,

begotten, not made, consubstantial with the Father;

through him all things were made.

For us men and for our salvation

he came down from heaven,

and by the Holy Spirit was incarnate of the Virgin Mary,

and became man.

For our sake he was crucified under Pontius Pilate,

he suffered death and was buried,

and rose again on the third day

in accordance with the Scriptures.

He ascended into heaven
and is seated at the right hand of the Father.
He will come again in glory
to judge the living and the dead
and his kingdom will have no end.

I believe in the Holy Spirit, the Lord, the giver of life,
who proceeds from the Father and the Son,
who with the Father and Son is adored and glorified,
who has spoken through the prophets.

I believe in one holy, catholic, and apostolic Church.
I confess one Baptism for the forgiveness of sins
and I look forward to the resurrection of the dead
and the life of the world to come. Amen.

Glory Be (Doxology)

This is a short prayer that Christians sometimes add to the end of psalms. It is prayed during the Rosary and usually follows the opening verse during the Liturgy of the Hours. It can be prayed at any time during the day.

Glory be to the Father

and to the Son

and to the Holy Spirit,

as it was in the beginning

is now, and ever shall be

world without end. Amen.

Hail Mary

The first two lines of this prayer are the words of the angel Gabriel to Mary, when he announces that she is with child (Luke 1:28). The second two lines are Elizabeth's greeting to Mary (Luke 1:42). The last four lines come to us from deep in history, from where and from whom we do not know. This prayer is part of the Rosary and is often used by Christians for personal prayer.

Hail, Mary, full of grace,

the Lord is with thee.

Blessed art thou among women

and blessed is the fruit of thy womb, Jesus.

Holy Mary, Mother of God,

pray for us sinners,

now and at the hour of our death.

Amen.

Grace before Meals

Families pray before meals in different ways. Some families make up a prayer in their own words, other families sing a prayer, and many families use this traditional formula. Teach your children to say this prayer while signing themselves with the cross.

Bless us, O Lord, and these thy gifts,

which we are about to receive from thy bounty,

through Christ our Lord.

Amen.

Grace after Meals

Teach your children to say this prayer after meals, while signing themselves with the cross. The part in brackets is optional.

We give thee thanks, for all thy benefits,

almighty God, who lives and reigns forever.

[And may the souls of the faithful departed,

through the mercy of God, rest in peace.]

Amen.